Transforming Conversations

The Bridge from Individual
Leadership to Organisational Change

IAN HARCUS

Published by Three Loops Ltd.

ISBN 978-1-8380256-1-8

CONTENTS

ACKNOWLEDGMENTS

My huge thanks and appreciation to Alexander Chenet, Kennard Wing, Jane Allen, Kirstin Irving and Neil Hollister for many conversations, suggestions, and detailed input to earlier drafts; to Mark Edwards, Chuck Palus and Peter Cooper for helpful and insightful conversations; to Martin Donnachie for sharing his experiences; and to Bill Torbert for his encouragement, support, pointers, and reviews of many drafts.

My further thanks to Bill Isaacs, Frederic Laloux and Mark Edwards for permission to quote from, respectively, their books *Dialogue and the Art of Thinking Together*, *Reinventing Organisations*, and *Organisational Transformation for Sustainability – An Integral Metatheory*; and to Bill Torbert for permission to quote from across his body of work.

Tables 5.2 and 5.3 are inspired by the Center for Creative Leadership's Leadership Culture Map, developed by Chuck Palus.

FOREWORD BY BILL TORBERT

How has Ian Harcus managed to take the example of a small cafe (as well as examples from Facebook, U.S. Steel, McKinsey, Tesla, and other major organisations) to produce the most usable primer I can imagine, to help managers and leaders in all sectors in transforming your outside-in understanding of "organisations" into an inside-out experience of "organising differently" through different kinds of conversations.

Strongly supported by a small community of inquiry (consisting of Jane Allen, Alexander Chenet, Kirstin Irving, and Kennard Wing), Harcus provides practitioners with detailed, step-by-step tables for the very different kinds of organisational conversations necessary to help any organisation evolve rather than stagnate.

All of which will lead readers who feel a sense of responsibility and adventurousness to want to pursue the avenues for further exploration of the "developmental way" that Harcus offers toward the end.

For while a good theory can be very practical, it can only become so if one in fact learns its practice, which I call "action inquiry". Conversational action inquiry can generate multiple personal and organisational transformations. Indeed, the developmental way can, fortunately, take a lifetime to learn and can earn you more success and deeper friendships than you imagined possible.

Bill Torbert
Boston, March 2020

EXECUTIVE SUMMARY

Organisational change initiatives have a notoriously poor track record. A McKinsey & Company article[1] states "the reported failure rate of large-scale change programs has hovered around 70 percent over many years." The authors go on to wonder "How many times have frontline managers told us things like 'we have undergone three transformations in the last eight years, and each time we were back where we started 18 months later'?"

This book introduces a different way to think about organisational performance and change. It identifies clear reasons why change initiatives fail so regularly, and offers a different approach to improve chances of success. It also aims to be practical: to help people in organisations find steps they can take to make their group more effective, responsive, and enjoyable.

The heart of the model refers to the kinds of conversations that take place in an organisation. For example, one group may find it hard to discuss new ideas; another may find it easy to discuss starting new activities, but harder to discuss stopping existing ones; a third may be at ease exploring underlying assumptions and goals.

The model claims that dynamics such as these are pivotal to any group's success. It proposes a series of developmental stages for these dynamics, where organisations moving to later stages acquire greater agility, resilience, and effectiveness by being able to have different kinds of conversations – a bit like an organisational operating system upgrade. The theory is called *developmental theory*, and the stages are called *organisational action-logics*.

One implication is that an organisation that never has conversations about how well it works as whole is unlikely to work well as a whole. Others include:

- Organisations able to evolve to their next organisational action-logic – where they have introduced a new kind of conversation and succeeded in embedding it in their culture – will likely see significant, lasting improvement in effectiveness and performance.
- Organisational redesigns – highly prevalent in the corporate world –

will likely fail to deliver significant, lasting improvement unless they also stimulate or enable development to a later action-logic. Conventional wisdom on corporate transformation is overlooking this effective lever of change.

- Many structures and processes – for example balanced scorecards, shared services models, self-organising teams, and the approaches described in Frederic Laloux's book *Reinventing Organisations* – only really flourish once an organisation has reached a particular action-logic. Attempts to impose a later-stage structure or process on an earlier stage organisation can cause dysfunction.

The model also offers a possible bridge between leadership development and organisational performance. If leadership training and coaching supports people introducing new kinds of conversations, the impact of these can be measured.

The model of organisational action-logics was developed by Bill Torbert in the 1980s and 90s, and is covered most comprehensively in his book *Action Inquiry*. This book is based on that work, and is in part a primer on organisational action logics. It aims to make the model easier to grasp, help people spot opportunities to work with it, and provide the practical tools for them to do so.

Part One aims to help people understand the different kinds of conversations that can take place, and their implications for the organisation and its interaction with the outside world. Part Two provides practical tools to help people apply it. Part Three provides more specialist, technical details.

---

[1] *Transformation with a Capital T*, McKinsey, 2016

PART ONE

A PRIMER ON THE MODEL

Primer

ONE

Introducing three cafes

To illustrate three materially different kinds of conversation, consider three cafes. These are *The Level Three (Incorporation)*, *The Level Five (Systematic Productivity)* and *The Level Seven (Collaborative Inquiry)*. Each represents a different organisational action-logic.

Figure 1.1

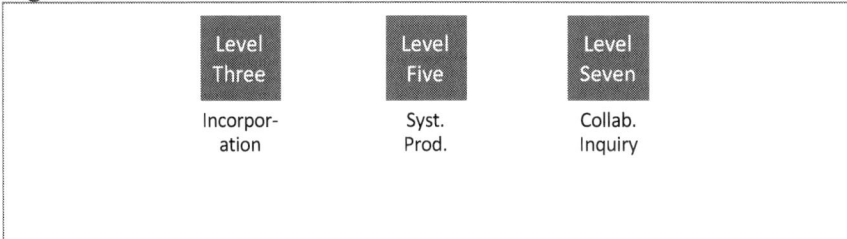

The defining characteristic of each cafe is what kinds of topics are discussable or undiscussable within its organisation. The cafes have different social dynamics, so a topic that can be raised and discussed in one cafe may be undiscussable within the social norms of another – see Table 1.1. Some topics may be undiscussable because they are unconscious or invisible, others because they are known but taboo. As will be shown over the next few pages, these boundaries between discussable and undiscussable topics have profound implications for the internal dynamics of the organisations, as well as how each one interacts with its external environment.

At *The Level Three (Incorporation)*, discussable subjects tend to be limited to social chitchat, and information exchanges required to carry out work, such as "where should I put this tray of muffins?" or "how do I operate the dishwasher?" The nature and design of the work itself are given, or undiscussable. Suggestions such as "why don't we store the muffins over there instead?" or "how about we sell that new brand of coffee they're advertising at the moment?" are likely to be dismissed, for example with words such as "you just get on with your job" or "that's not how we do things around here."

Table 1.1: Discussable and undiscussable topics

Type of cafe	What's discussable and discussed	What's undiscussable or undiscussed
"The Level Three" (Incorporation)	Information exchanges as necessary to perform the work Social chitchat	Changes to the work done or how it is carried out
"The Level Five" (Systematic Productivity)	As Three, plus what work is to be done and how it is to be carried out	Changes to the goal, to the structure or purpose of the organisation
"The Level Seven" (Collaborative Inquiry)	As Five, plus the goal itself, the structure and purpose of the organisation	Will inherit undiscussables from wider society, perhaps aspects of sex, illness, mental health, death.

Not much changes in *The Level Three (Incorporation)*. They have their way of doing things, and neither seek nor welcome suggestions to do things differently. In this organisation, feedback or suggestions are seen as a threat, or perhaps as a cause for shame. It makes the group uncomfortable, so they either ignore it or become defensive. This means that *The Level Three (Incorporation)* has very limited abilities to learn or adapt to change.

Level Five (Systematic Productivity)

The Level Five (Systematic Productivity) operates at a later organisational action-logic where the work and how it is carried out is now discussable. This ability to discuss "doing things differently" allows the organisation to:

- Set and measure goals for a different future, goals such as sales, profits, stock wastage, cleanliness, customer satisfaction, or employee turnover.
- Seek feedback and improvement ideas from customers, employees, other cafes, magazine articles, etc.
- Review performance against goals and explore ways to improve, e.g., through morning team meetings on customer feedback and cleanliness, monthly meetings on sales and profits, quarterly meetings on products sold, and employee turnover.

(Incidentally, *The Level Five* has several outlets. There's nothing to stop a single cafe operating at *Level Five (Systematic Productivity)*, but it later becomes helpful to the story for it to have several outlets.)

The Level Five (Systematic Productivity) isn't just willing to try doing things differently, it has put in place processes to manage change. For example, it may have a process to manage the range of products it sells. Through this process, it evaluates new products in the market, tracks products it's already launched, and evaluates rising sellers, falling sellers, and under-performing products. *The Level Five* knows which products it should promote more strongly and which it should discontinue – it is fully aware of the dangers of having too many products, with the subsequent risk of confusing staff and customers, and having too much stock. This cafe easily handles suggestions like "how about we sell that new brand of coffee they're advertising at the moment?" – such suggestions slot into its regular review processes.

The following examples suggest an organisation has reached this level:

- Amazon CEO Jeff Bezos has spoken about his role of making sure that Amazon fails quickly, in the sense that the faster an experiment either proves its success or fails, the better for the company.
- Jack Welch wrote of his time as CEO of GE that "best practice sharing just happens at GE".
- The Procter & Gamble recruitment process emphasises hiring people who set and work towards goals.
- McKinsey & Company expects its consultants to set learning objectives for each assignment.
- Any organisation that has regular cycles of Plan-Do-Review, Plan-Do-Check-Act, Six Sigma or comparable continual improvement processes.

The common thread running through these examples is that improving performance is embedded in "how we do things around here."

What's not discussable in *Systematic Productivity* organisations are suggestions that involve a fundamental change in mindset. This might involve a complete change in approach, goal, or to the identity of the organisation, such as:

- Adopting a structure such as self-organising teams, where teams have a high degree of autonomy, can choose their own approach, and make decisions previously taken by senior management.
- Introducing bold social goals, such as donating 30% of profits to local good causes, or offering to employ homeless people to help them re-establish themselves in society.
- If the cafe has a down-to-earth identity summed up with the phrase "everyday food for everyday folks," the suggestion to open a new outlet serving fancier, more expensive food.

It's useful at this stage to introduce some terminology. *Single-loop learning* means keeping the same goal and mindset, but changing the work to achieve the goal more effectively; *double-loop learning* involves changing the goal or the mindset as well as the work. See Table 1.2. Double-loop learning often involves a change of identity and some pain or regret in letting go of the original identity.

There aren't always hard and fast rules about what is single- or double-loop. For example, for one carpenter, starting to use a new kind of power tool with a slightly different technique could be single-loop learning. For a different carpenter, who prides him or herself on only using traditional tools and techniques, starting to use a power tool would be double-loop, with some possible regret at the loss of identity as a traditional craftsperson.

Table 1.2: Comparing Single- and Double-Loop learning

	Single-loop learning	Double-loop learning
Summary	New approach to tasks that is easily absorbed by the existing mindset and identity	Change in fundamental assumptions or strategy that challenges existing mindset or identity.
Clues	Unlikely to be any pain or regret in letting go.	Reasonable chance of some pain or regret in letting go
Example (carpenter)	Carpenter who already uses power tools learning how to use a new, unfamiliar power tool	Traditional carpenter with pride in using only traditional tools abandoning that identity and starting to use power tools.

Likewise, for a cafe that already serves premium food, introducing wine or cocktails could be single-loop. But for a cafe with an "everyday folk" identity, it would be double-loop involving some pain in the loss of that identity. At *Level Five (Systematic Productivity)*, an organisation has institutionalised single-loop learning, but would struggle with double-loop.

Level Seven (Collaborative Inquiry)

Turning to *Level Seven*, these organisations have mastered double-loop changes of the kind described above. In such organisations "openness to questioning exists, assumptions are tested, seeming mistakes are rarely punished but are a basis for further learning, new knowledge is shared, and new knowledge is gained collaboratively" (*Action Inquiry* p122). Such an organisation "truly encourages the practice of developmental action inquiry among all its members and is actively open to re-examining and transforming its own assumptions about its environment, its structure and its strategies" (*Action*

Inquiry p148).

In *Level Seven* organisations, it has become socially acceptable to raise and discuss radical changes to goals, structure, and identity. This means it is now possible to evaluate and implement changes that hurt, that involve some loss of identity, or that have the potential to cause uproar among some stakeholder groups.

By way of example, Amazon used to be an ecommerce provider that sold its own goods. In 1999, it introduced z-shops, which allowed other merchants to sell their products on Amazon's website. Later it integrated z-shops with the main site, so that competitors' products were shown alongside Amazon's products. Imagine the potential for uproar and confusion among Amazon employees: "why on earth are we helping our competitors?" or "we are allowing our competitors to undercut us *on our own site*. What are we thinking?"

Jack Welch introduced ideas such as *GE workouts*, which required senior management to respond quickly to suggestions from operational employees (possible reaction: "hang on, who calls the shots around here?"), and *boundarylessness,* which introduced a different way of collaborating internally between functions and divisions, but also externally with suppliers and customers (possible reaction: "wait a minute, why are we sharing all this confidential information with our suppliers?").

These are all examples of double-loop learning, change that may hurt because it affects how people think about themselves or because of a need to let go of an old mindset – a mindset where senior managers don't have any obligations to operational employees, or where an organisation takes an adversarial relationship with suppliers. This is not to say that Amazon or GE reached *Collaborative Inquiry*, but rather that embedding the ability to consider and implement radical changes like these comes only at *Level Seven*.

Level Seven organisations can also engage in constructive dialogue with opponents, or even groups who are acting as enemies. For example, Warren Buffet sought out Wall Street analysts who had published a negative recommendation on Berkshire Hathaway stock. He planned to invite them to Berkshire Hathaway's annual shareholder meeting to present their rationale for the negative outlook.

TWO

Experiments: the journey from *incorporation* to *systematic productivity*

The cafe *The Level Three (Incorporation)* is characterised by a set way of doing things and an inability to discuss new ideas. Table 2.1 lists its strengths and limitations.

Table 2.1: Strengths and limitations of *Level Three (Incorporation)*

Level Three: **strengths to celebrate**

- Achieving and maintaining viability, e.g., meeting the needs of customers, employees, shareholders and keeping the show on the road.
- Honouring heritage or tradition, a sense of loyalty and belonging, a sense of how things are done around here.

Level Three: **signs it might be time to move on**

- The external environment is changing, but the business isn't, e.g.: "Customers don't seem to value our tradition so much these days" or "Businesses like ours are losing out to a new type of business / product / trend."
- The leaders want more ideas and options raised in team meetings.
- The organisation is a team, function, or division within a wider organisation, and there is feedback or clues it needs to adapt more rapidly to the changing needs of that wider organisation.

Clues an organisation is at this stage include:
- Unlikely to be much in the way of a management information (MI) pack. Any success measures will likely have been mandated externally, e.g., legal or parent company requirements.
- Unlikely to be many change initiatives beyond those prompted externally, e.g., a supplier discontinued a product, or management cut the budget for an activity or told them to start doing something.

- Little meaningful review of performance. Meetings have a ritual, "going through the motions" aspect to them. Anything remotely uncomfortable will be avoided altogether or tackled in private.

The cafe gets a new management team who are more ambitious and innovative, and promote the discussion of new ideas. (Chapters 5-7 looks at how they might do that.) The cafe is evolving to the *Experiments* action-logic.

Figure 2.1

Level Three	Level Four	Level Five		Level Seven
Incorpor-ation	Experi-ments	Syst. Prod.		Collab. Inquiry

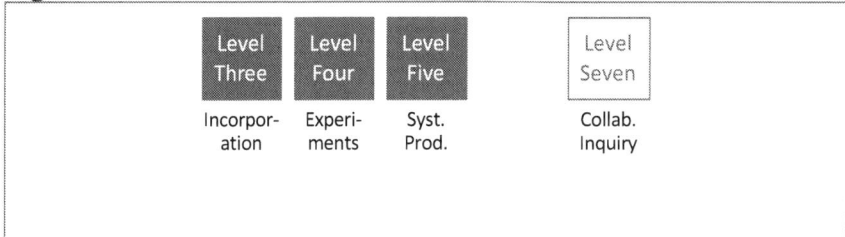

Here is how their experiments might evolve over a couple of years: the renamed *The Level Four (Experiments)* starts selling that new brand of coffee that's being advertised; then converts the back yard to a garden terrace; next starts selling alcoholic drinks; later sets up a BBQ shack in the garden terrace; and then expands to a second location on the other side of town. The new location starts selling different kinds of food, and evolves into more of a bar with food than a cafe. They then open new locations in different towns, bringing the total, over these two years, to five outlets.

In a typical *Experiments* organisation, the managers of each of the five outlets would have considerable autonomy to make their own decisions as long as they hit their revenue and profit targets. They choose what brands to sell, which suppliers to use, and decide on their own hiring practices. Advantages of this include clear authority and accountability, local decision-making that takes into account local needs, and a structure that's fairly straightforward to manage. Cafe and bar managers who deliver on their revenue and profit targets are rewarded with bonuses; those that underperform are replaced.

This stage also has limitations. If each outlet buys different branded supplies from different suppliers, then the business as a whole is missing out on the best deals. There is limited sharing of ideas, experiences, and best practices between bars. Local staff must be jacks of all trades, doing everything for themselves, even though they'll likely lack the skills to perform them all well.

Experiments organisations can tend towards fragmentation and decentralisation. A *Level Four (Experiments)* business can become less of a single business, and more a federation of different businesses. Table 2.2 lists its strengths and limitations. Clues an organisation is at this stage include:

- Company-level MI packs will likely just measure financials and perhaps a few operational measures. At the operational level, there will be a tendency to measure what is easy rather than what is useful. MI packs likely to have a haphazard quality: lacking important measures (such as customer satisfaction), but full of stuff that's ultimately not useful for managing the business (e.g., Twitter followers).
- Lots of examples of new initiatives and projects that improve the business. Less likely to discontinue activities unless forced by external circumstances. Limited ability to manage the overall portfolio of improvement initiatives, so there may be too many, and they may pull in too many different directions
- Key meetings will contain lots of information updates, status of measures, progress on projects. Discussions less likely get to the root cause of issues.

Table 2.2: Strengths and limitations of *Level Four (Experiments)*

Level Four: strengths to celebrate

- Establishing the social norm that it is OK to suggest doing things differently.
- Being able to improve, innovate, and evolve.

Level Four: signs it might be time to move on

- The organisation is spread too thinly: too many products, services, activities, improvement initiatives.
- Fragmentation: the business is organised in silos. These may be in some way better, but make the organisation more expensive – a problem if customers or external stakeholders aren't willing to pay the premium for this.
- The organisational is complex: too many suppliers, different IT systems, different ways of doing the same thing.
- Performance targets in one part have adverse effects on other parts of the organisation.
- The whole is less than the sum of the parts, and this matters.

At this point, the leadership team might think something along the lines of "whoa, this is getting out of control. Our five outlets between them sell six different brands of coffee, four of cola, have three different till systems, five different hiring and staff bonus policies. And we have no central visibility of purchase prices, stock levels, or what products are selling well. What's more, we are not sharing any knowledge or best practices between outlets. We could manage things so much better than this."

The above remark introduces a fundamentally new kind of conversation. The shift from *Three (Incorporation)* to *Four (Experiments)* represented adding the ability to discuss and implement new ideas. The shift from *Four (Experiments)* to *Five (Systematic Productivity)* represents adding the ability to discuss the efficiency and effectiveness of the overall whole; to discuss – based on a greater understanding of cause and effect – changes to the organisation that benefit the whole even if they disadvantage one part. It also adds the ability to openly discuss stopping programmes and activities.

These discussions on the effectiveness of the whole, and being equally at ease starting *and stopping* activities, might result in actions such as following:

- Standardising on a common set of products to be sold across all cafes and bars.
- Centralising purchasing and supplier management to negotiate better prices from a smaller number of suppliers.
- Implementing common till and stock management systems, giving greater visibility of stock and sales by product.
- Using the information from the common information technology (IT) systems to identify patterns in sales, spot opportunities for improvement, and manage the business "as a whole" rather than outlet by outlet.
- Standardising policies on hiring, wages, and bonuses. Recruiting a central HR specialist to help recruit new staff. Implementing a central system to support outlets when staff are ill or on leave.

Table 2.3 lists the strengths of *Systematic Productivity*. Clues an organisation is at this stage include:

- It tracks a range of success measures, not just financial but also customer satisfaction, employee satisfaction, quality, and so on. Also understands cause and effect, so they will track the operational causes of the high-level success criteria.
- It measures what's useful, not just what's easy. MI pack structured in a logical way that provides a thorough health check of the business based on an understanding of cause and effect.
- Meaningful targets are in place for all key measures, perhaps guided by external benchmarking.
- Decisions regarding change are more likely to start with a high-level assessment of what is important to the business, and what the priority improvement areas are. A smaller number of initiatives will then be selected from a larger pool of possibilities based on their relevant to these high-level goals. There will be clear "bigger picture" that was lacking at *Experiments*.
- Able to manage the overall portfolio of initiatives, focusing on ensuring a smaller number of high-impact projects are successful. Able to stop less useful projects.

- Open discussion on goals and targets, underperformance, root causes of underperformance, and exploration of improvement actions.
- Little concern about blame, instead concern about fixing and improving things.

Table 2.3: Strengths of *Level Five (Systematic Productivity)*

Level Five: strengths to celebrate

- Being a really good organisation, one that is probably among the best in its industry or field.
- Understanding cause and effect – comprehensive measures in place not just for the desirable and obvious effects (growth, profit, etc.) but also all the underlying operational process excellence that enables them.
- Being able to both create and destroy: launch new products and kill underperforming ones; create new initiatives, stop less useful ones. As a result, being able to innovate while keeping things simple (compared to the previous level which would tend to innovate at the expense of complexity).

The ways an action-logic manifest itself will vary according to an organisation's size, culture, profit or not-for-profit, and so on. Table 2.4 illustrates how the dynamics of *Systematic Productivity* might take shape in three different organisations.

Downsides of *Systematic Productivity*

As conversations about the efficiency and effectiveness of the overall whole become more prevalent in an organisation, its structure and processes will likely evolve. It will evolve from the typical characteristics of *Experiments* (silos, fragmentation) to the typical characteristics of *Systematic Productivity* (standardisation, shared services, more targets and measures). This evolution comes with at least three potential downsides.

First is the potential for efficiency at the expense of dehumanisation. The HR manager used to be two minutes down the corridor, now he or she is in a shared services function in another office, or maybe in a call centre in the Philippines. The manager of *The Level Four* could decide to sell a new brand of coffee, the manager of *The Level Five* is told what to sell.

Consider the case of how school lunches are prepared in a district of 50 schools. In a typical *Experiments* structure, each school hires local people, who can buy from local suppliers. In a typical *Systematic Productivity* structure, all food is prepared centrally, and possibly industrially. Local communities lose skilled jobs – now they just need someone to reheat the frozen food – and local suppliers lose revenue.

Table 2.4: *Systematic Productivity* in different kinds of organisations

A 200-employee business	A 200-employee business operating at *Systematic Productivity* should have a reasonably comprehensive MI pack. The business has a vision of success (going beyond financials to include measures such as customer satisfaction and employee satisfaction) and, based on an understanding of cause and effect, tracks the operational enablers of success. It has targets in place for all key measures, perhaps supported by external benchmarking. (All this will likely create scores of PowerPoint slides per review cycle.)
A three-person pop-up food stall that visits different fairs and festivals	The team keeps an eye on how consumer demand for their stall compares against the others. They invite customer feedback, both verbally and with a sign showing their email and twitter handle. They inspect the other stalls to see what they can learn from them, both on how they operate and how they promote themselves. After each festival, they have a short team discussion to review how it all went, what they learned from anything new they tried out, and agree on goals for next time. There are no PowerPoint slides, and indeed they seldom document any of this.
A 20,000-employee business of multiple business units or geographic units	A multi-business organisation operating at *Systematic Productivity* takes action to generate efficiencies across business units. This might include standardising on common IT systems and processes, mandating standard operational success measures and benchmarking, and centralising support functions such as IT, finance, and HR.

The second downside is the potential for significant loss of efficiency if the shared or outsourced service does not itself operate at *Systematic Productivity*. When the overall group structure is at *Experiments*, then if the school leaders do not like the lunches, they can change them; if the cafe managers do not like the coffee brands, they can change them; if the business unit leader has problems with HR or IT support, they can fix it.

If the shared service – the central catering function, the drinks purchasing team, or the outsourced IT/HR function – is able to listen to, discuss and act on feedback, this should be fine, but if they haven't themselves reached *Level Five (Systematic Productivity)*, they probably won't. The business/school/cafe will then be stuck with a support function that doesn't meet their needs, and will be powerless to do anything about it. This illustrates a fundamental theme of this work, that imposing a structure or process characteristic of a later organisational action-logic on an organisation that has not reached that stage can cause dysfunction.

Third is the risk of overuse of standardisation, measurement, and targets. School head teachers who are told not just what lessons must be taught, but also how they must be taught, and face an overwhelming quantity of measures and targets that do not help them improve performance, are experiencing this downside. (Chapter 2.2 of Laloux's *Reinventing Organisations* has an instructive case study on this problem at Buurtzorg, a neighbourhood nursing organisation in the Netherlands.)

THREE

Social network: the journey from *systematic productivity* to *collaborative inquiry*

By this stage in its evolution, the cafe and bar group, *The Level Five (Systematic Productivity)*, is a huge success: it leads its industry on profit margins, growth, customer satisfaction, and employee retention. It now has 15 outlets, and plans to double that to 30 within the next two years. It has a strong corporate culture – company values drive hiring, for example – and there is a clear sense of what kind of person thrives at *The Level Five*.

Figure 3.1

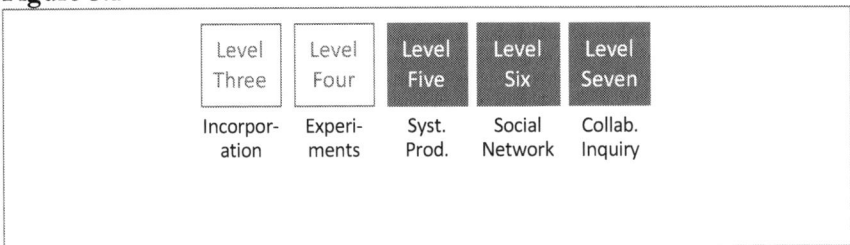

Level Three	Level Four	Level Five	Level Six	Level Seven
Incorporation	Experiments	Syst. Prod.	Social Network	Collab. Inquiry

There is, however, a sense of unease among its leadership team. (Table 3.1 lists some of the limitations of *Systematic Productivity*.) They start asking themselves questions such as: do they really want to create just another large, slightly faceless corporate chain? Do they really want to live in a society where large chains dominate the cafe and bar sectors? Do they personally want a society where businesses just focus on profits, or where they also take seriously their contributions to and impact on their local communities? If creating this organisation is to be part of *their lives' work*, what kind of organisation would be true to their lives, and worthy of being *their lives' work*?

These questions introduce a fundamentally new kind of conversation: that of exploring underlying assumptions and mindsets. In this instance, they are challenging assumptions about the goal and identity of the organisation, including the importance of growth, profits and efficiency. Functions within a larger organisation could have similar conversations, for instance purchasing might challenge a mindset that relies primarily on aggressive price negotiation to get the best value from suppliers.

Table 3.1: Limitations of *Level Five (Systematic Productivity)*

Level Five: signs it might be time to move on

- The organisation is facing one or more losing (or at least unwinnable) battles: problems or challenges that haven't gone away, and which, if the organisation is really honest with itself, show no signs of going away. Any high levels of optimisation, determination, and "we can do this, team" enthusiasm were equally high three-to-five years ago.

- The emphasis on success measures is creating undesirable side effects, e.g., the league tables of schools mean teachers stop teaching the subject, and start teaching to the exams.

- Officially the organisation is performing well, and the numbers look good. Talking to different groups of stakeholders, however, yields an ambiguous or different picture. Some groups of stakeholders are unhappy, dissatisfied, or otherwise poorly served by the system.

- The owners, board, or leaders are interested in exploring their assumptions and challenging themselves on what kind of organisation they personally want to create, what kind of society they personally want to live in, what kind of organisation would be true to their lives, and be worthy of being their lives' work.

- The efficiency juggernaut can be dehumanising. This bothers the leadership team, but they aren't sure what, if anything, they can do about it.

The management team's discussions are wide-ranging, and not always conclusive, but a consensus emerges that they do not want to become another Starbucks or McDonalds. This is not a conversation about business strategy and profit maximisation – that would be a *Systematic Productivity* conversation. It is far more personal and intimate: a conversation about what kind of organisation is worthy of being *their lives' work*. They might, for example, examine what kind of society they personally want to live in, and what actions their organisation should take to be consistent with their vision of society.

These discussions might result in actions such as following:

- Giving local teams considerably more autonomy, and encouraging them to make their cafe or bar more individual, and reflect local needs. Encouraging local teams to have similar conversations.

- Accepting non-conformity, including accepting ways of dressing and hairstyles that wouldn't have been tolerated previously.

- Allowing managers who have been with the company for at least three years to take secondments to local charity / not-for-profit organisations.
- Donating a proportion of profits to local good causes.

This journey from *Five* to *Seven* has parallels with that of *Three* to *Five* – see Table 3.2.

Table 3.2: Parallels between the *Experiments* and *Social Network* journeys

	Journey from three to five	Journey from five to seven
Start point	• Unwillingness or inability to branch out or experiment.	• Unwillingness or inability to explore underlying assumptions and mindsets.
Middle	• Willingness to branch out and experiment. • Inability to prevent excessive branching out and experimentation.	• Willingness to try out new approaches with different fundamental mindsets or assumptions. • Limited ability to resolve conflict between mindsets.
End point	• Ability to manage the experiments so they work well together within an efficient whole.	• Ability to manage and integrate differing or incompatible mindsets.

After three years of these different kinds of experiments – some successful, others not – the cafe has renamed itself *The Level Six (Social Network)*. It has three regions – Northern, Southern and Western – each with about 10 outlets, and a shared services function that handles finance, IT, HR, supplier management, and marketing. (*Social Networks* keep *Systematic Productivity's* ability to discuss the efficiency of the whole.)

The leadership of Northern Region is highly driven. They set bold goals for revenue growth, profitability, customer satisfaction, and have performance measures in place for everything. They lead the group on pretty much every benchmark. Their bonus structure gives high rewards to cafe and bar managers who hit their targets. Advocates of Jack Welch's approach at GE, they routinely fire the lowest performing 10% of their workforce.

Western Region is more relaxed and inclusive, but still performing. Their leadership team shares 25% of profits with staff, and donates another 25% to local good causes. Southern region also performs well, and achieved national fame with its scheme for employing recently-released prisoners to help them re-establish themselves in society. Meanwhile, the shared services function has decided to package up its IT, finance, HR, supplier management, and marketing services, and start selling them to third-party cafes, bars, hotels, and restaurants.

The story so far illustrates what is meant by different mindsets and identities. Consider the potential for uproar: Northern Region feels it is busting its gut to maximise profits and is incensed that Western Region is "just giving half away." And don't get them started on Southern Region's prisoner scheme. Western Region is outraged and embarrassed by Northern's "brutal employment policies," and feels these don't just damage the brand, but are unethical too.

All three regions are irritated by the shared services function's selling services to third parties. "They're helping our competitors, for heaven's sake." Unions and the media are challenging the group hard on why Western Region's employees get 25% of the profits, and other employees don't. "It's not fair." On social media, a campaign to boycott the group goes viral.

Table 3.3: *The Level Six (Social Network)*

Vision	A flourishing independent – and independently-minded – cafe and bar sector.
Mission	Enable independent cafes and bars to thrive against large corporate chains.
Strategy	Provide independent and independently-minded cafe and bar owners with: • Efficient infrastructure – IT systems, finance, HR, purchasing, etc. – so they can compete against the big chains. • Flexible financing and ownership options, including majority or minority ownership. • Advice, mentoring, and specialist skills – a network of experience. • Moral support and encouragement on the spirit of independence in the cafe and bar sectors.
Structure	• An overall holding company that owns some of the cafes and bars outright, has a majority stake in some, a minority stake in others. • Local management of existing cafes and bars are given the option to take shared ownership of their outlet. • Willingness to take a minority or majority stake in new outlets. • The shared services company is owned and governed by the outlets, so each one has one share and vote in how it is run.

Tensions like these are probably unsustainable, and illustrate some of the instability at *Social Network*. The group realises this, and its leadership teams debate these issues over several months without resolution. The leadership of Northern Region grow increasingly frustrated, and eventually suggest that Northern splits off from the group through a management buy-out. Patience exhausted, they further say they will resign if this request is not granted.

Over the following six months, the group has several crisis meetings, concludes that a traditional single corporate entity is too rigid a structure for a *Level Six (Social Network)* organisation, agrees to Northern Region's management buyout, and initiates a review of mission, structure, and strategy. One consultancy project and several off-site workshops later, *The Level Six (Social Network)* reinvents itself as shown in Table 3.3. This new identity is a result of double-loop learning, with the potential for pain and regret at the loss of the previous identity.

The rationale for all this is that, considered as a whole, the independent cafe and bar sector has a structure characteristic of *Experiments*, and will find it difficult to compete against large chains, which have the cost advantages of *Systematic Productivity*. *The Level Six (Social Network)*'s strategy and structure is designed to support independent-spirited cafe and bar owners who have their own individual vision. It offers them the efficiency of *Systematic Productivity* without its depersonalisation.

At this point, it's worth contrasting the autonomy enjoyed by local unit managers in different organisations – see Table 3.4.

Managers in *The Level Six* are in an unusual situation: they can choose their cafe or bar's name, decor and furnishings, but are told what till system to use and who to bank with; and they must agree to be benchmarked, but can totally ignore the results of the benchmarking study. There are two related reasons for this.

First, a *Social Network* must retain the efficiency and best practice sharing of *Systematic Productivity*. The common till systems, for example, allow the central team to measure, compare, create league tables, and spot patterns and opportunities for efficiency. Managers receive reports each month comparing their outlet's performance with the others, and highlighting successes and failures across the group, for example with new products launches. Without all this, the organisation has regressed to a structure characteristic of *Experiments* rather than advanced to a structure characteristic of *Social Network*.

Second, the mission of the group – enable independent cafes and bars to thrive against large corporate chains – requires these compulsory policies. To thrive against corporates, the independent outlets need to become more efficient, and to become more efficient, they need a structure such as *The Level Six (Social Network)*.

The Level Six has a collegiate atmosphere. There is a sense of togetherness that comes from the shared vision and mission. The leadership team encourages and maintains this with initiatives such as a mentoring programme that assigns new outlet owners a more senior mentor, ad-hoc task forces across cafes and bars on various issues, social forums for people to get to know each other, and with much discussion and listening to keep the shared vision and mission alive.

Table 3.4: Local unit autonomy in different large organisations

Level Four (Experiments)	• Core purpose – e.g., maximising sales and profits – is assumed and non-negotiable.
	• Depending on the organisation, other parameters may be defined as non-negotiable, e.g., sales targets for a strategic new product launch by the group.
	• Other than that, a unit operating within a *Level Four* group will likely have a high degree of autonomy if they are hitting financial targets, as group management probably has little interest in operational matters.
Level Five (Systematic Productivity)	• At the extreme, pretty much everything may be defined and specified as group-wide standards and processes. Local managers are there to execute, not design or make policy decisions.
Level Six (Social Network)	Will vary by organisation, but in this example, local managers in *The Level Six*:
	• Can choose their purpose, including profit or non-profit, and any kind of broader social aim.
	• Have full choice over the cafe or bar's name, décor, furnishings, target customer, price point, HR policies, wage policies, and so on.
	• Are expected to use group-managed suppliers for at least 70% of goods sold, though exceptions to this can be negotiated if there is good cause.
	• Must use group IT systems, i.e., they have no choice over till technology, stock management and financial accounting systems, or HR systems. Also have no choice over their bank or auditor.
	• Must participate in group benchmarking and best practice sharing programmes (though it's optional whether they pay any attention to the results).

Frederic Laloux describes how later stage organisations "unleash unprecedented energy and creativity" (*Reinventing Organisations*, p189). Readers are invited to consider, with reference to Table 3.4, whether they would rather work in *The Level Five* or *The Level Six*, and which they would prefer to open a cafe or bar in their neighbourhood.

Table 3.5 lists the strengths and limitations of a *Social Network*. Clues an organisation is at this stage include:

- It should really have similar MI to *Systematic Productivity*, but how they talk about their measures will be different. At *Systematic Productivity*, people are likely to define themselves by the numbers, whereas at *Social Network*, the numbers matter, but are not the be all and end all.

- Likely to have a story beyond the numbers, and to take initiatives that improve things in ways that might not be reflected in the numbers. Likely also to be aware of the dangers of measurement, and may stop measuring some things for this reason.

- A good *Social Network* should keep some aspects of *Systematic Productivity*, but the emphasis will switch towards grass roots initiatives, ideally supported by some central infrastructure.

- More likely to encourage decentralised initiatives to see what new patterns emerge as a result of deliberately looser control

- Key meetings should keep *Systematic Productivity*'s open discussion about results. A *Social Network* is more likely to discuss what the measures overlook, success beyond the measures, changing the measures to make them more useful, or discarding them.

Table 3.5: Strengths and limitations of *Level Six (Social Network)*

Level Six: **strengths to celebrate**

- Resolving the efficiency-humanity paradox that eluded *Experiments* and *Systematic Productivity*.
- Being the voice of humanity and individuality in today's organisational climate (of transformation from *Experiments* to *Systematic Productivity*) where that voice badly needs to be heard.
- Operating at the leading edge of organisational levels at this time.

Level Six: **signs it might be time to move on**

- The leadership team perceives that the structure and strategy of the *Level Six* organisation is hindering its ability to realise its vision and mission (e.g., see CEO speech towards the end the next section).

Onwards to *Level Seven (Collaborative Inquiry)*

The group now has stakes in 120 outlets, typically owning between 20% and 80% of each. It appoints a new CEO, a CEO who was manager/co-owner of a cluster of *The Level Six's* outlets.

The new CEO calls a meeting of the cafe and bar co-owners and other senior managers. Here are extracts from her opening remarks:

"I joined this organisation six years ago, and have been a manager of at least one cafe or bar for nearly all of that time. I love this organisation. I love the autonomy that each of us has to develop our own visions, our own unique outlets. I love that in an age of standardisation, we offer our customers individual and unique experiences. And I love that we've found a special way to help an embattled independent sector thrive against the chains. These factors are why I joined, why I've stayed, and why I'm thrilled to be your CEO.

"Yet I worry about our future, and initiated this meeting to begin a discussion about our future. I worry that certain aspects of our culture, structure, and strategy get in the way of our achieving our vision and mission. Let me give you three examples.

"We have a horror of chains, and long may that continue. But this means we can be slow to replicate success. Three years ago, we opened *Bill's Bar*. It's been an outstanding success, but our horror of chains meant we didn't copy it. Several of our competitors have replicated our *Bill's Bar* formula, and one of those competitors is turning it into a chain. I'm not saying we should start a *Bill's Bar* chain, but are we being true to our mission if we make things this easy for our competitors? I'd like to hear your ideas this afternoon about how we might respond differently on this issue.

"Second, I valued the independence of my cafes and bars, and I know you all do, too. The thing is, I was so scared of losing that independence that sometimes I didn't speak out when I should. I suggest that as a group, we can be too reluctant to speak out and challenge each other – because we don't want other people speaking out and challenging us.

"As a result, I made many mistakes that I think people in this room could have helped me avoid. And I've seen some of you make mistakes that maybe I could have helped avoid. For me, this as part of a wider issue: we find it too convenient to duck conflict and disagreement, and hide in our own little islands. I'm hoping we can explore ways to strengthen how we work together while keeping that independence we all value so much.

"Third, our strategy is currently the sum of 120 or so individual decisions. We do little, if any, direction setting as an overall organisation. As a result, there are several large urban areas where we have no presence. We are behind on our digital experience – some of you are excellent on digital, but on the whole our competitors are stronger on things like Wi-Fi, charging points for customer devices, online reservations, and social media. We are behind the curve here and this worries me. Can we find ways to keep the advantages of local decision-making, while being more attentive to our business as a whole?

"Our mission is to help an independent sector thrive against the big corporates. I think the three examples I've just given show weak points where we could do better – you might have other examples, or you might disagree, and I'd love to hear your thoughts if you do. I've a few ideas about what we might do, but my main aim this morning is to understand your thinking and hear your ideas."

The above remarks are intended to illustrate several new kinds of conversation that mark the transformation to *Level Seven*. Torbert writes in *Managing the Corporate Dream:*

"At the *Collaborative Inquiry* stage, organisations not only produce goods or services but do so in ways whereby members continually reexplore the authority and legitimacy of the organisation's various structures, strategies and systems, with a regular process for amending them. The organisation *is* no longer any particular structure. It *has* structures. And it has inquiry systems *for* restructuring, and it is these with which it identifies more closely.

"The organisation at this stage of development deliberately fosters inquiry about its mission and about whether its structure, operations, and social outcomes are consistent with its mission and are beneficial. In other words, the question of whether the organisation functions so as to make the corporate dream come true begins, for the first time, to become explicit and to be tested as part of the regular functioning of the organisation." (p119)

Frederic Laloux researched what *Level Seven* organisations, which he calls *Teal Organisations* (teal as in the colour), look like in practice. His book *Reinventing Organisation*s presents common structures and processes found in his study of 12 Teal Organisations. He writes:

"The case studies of pioneer Teal Organisations researched for this book reveal three major breakthroughs:

- "**Self-management:** Teal Organisations have found the key to operate effectively, even at a large scale, with a system based on peer relationships, without the need for either hierarchy or consensus.

- "**Wholeness:** Organisations have always been places that encourage people to show up with a narrow 'professional' self and to check other parts of the self at the door. They often require us to show a masculine resolve, to display determination and strength, and to hide doubts and vulnerability. Rationality rules as king, while the emotional, intuitive, and spiritual parts of ourselves often feel unwelcome, out of place. Teal Organisations have developed a consistent set of practices that invite us to reclaim our inner wholeness and bring all of who we are to work.

- "**Evolutionary purpose:** Teal Organisations are seen as having a life and sense of direction of their own. Instead of trying to predict and control the future, members of the organisation are invited to listen in and understand what the organisation wants to become, what purpose it wants to serve.

"Each of these breakthroughs manifests itself through a number of concrete, day-to-day practices that depart – sometimes subtly, sometimes radically – from the traditionally accepted management methods." (*Reinventing Organisations*, pp 56-57)

These "concrete day-to-day practices" include "self-organising teams… minimum (or no) plans and budgets… [elimination of staff functions so] most such functions performed by teams themselves… peer-based processes for individual performance… regular time devoted to bring to light and address conflicts… all information available in real-time to all, including about company financials and compensation… strategy emerges organically from the collective intelligence of self-managing employees… no sales targets" and many others (*Reinventing Organisations*, pp 327-331).

FOUR

Examples of change

This section contains stories of change described through the lens of action-logics. They aim to illustrate the importance of conversational dynamics to organisational change initiatives.

Organisation A is a group of a dozen or so businesses, whose culture was estimated to be spread across *Incorporation*, *Experiments* and *Systematic Productivity*. Its CEO sponsored an internal quality management / business excellence programme based on the European Foundation for Quality Management (EFQM) model. This model has five enablers of performance (leadership, people, strategy, partnership & resources, and processes, products & services) and four result areas (people results, customer results, society results, and business results).

The programme used a maturity model for the five enablers and four result areas. Each enabler was broken into sub-categories: leadership, for example, might include a sub-category on how vision and mission were defined with input from different stakeholder groups, and another on how they were communicated across the business. There were five maturity levels, with a brief description of what being at that level involved for each sub-category. The result areas had similar maturity levels based on whether performance measures had been put in place, whether targets had been set and met, what the long-term trends were, and whether they'd been benchmarked against external companies.

The leadership team of each business was asked to self-assess against the maturity levels, and provide evidence to justify their self-assessment. They received a score against their assessment, and so could compare their performance against other businesses in the group, and previous years if available. They were then asked to agree a plan to improve.

The leadership teams found the entire process extremely valuable. They tended to take a day or two out of their schedules to do the assessment and then discuss the improvement plan. They found this an opportunity to step back from the day-to-day running of the business, and think more broadly and strategically about fundamentals. The maturity model and EFQM framework gave them a logical agenda to follow, and one which showed them what good companies do, as well as a practical path for improvement. It forced them to have new types of conversation. The scores appealed to their competitive natures, and the whole process had an element of fun.

Organisation A grew sales, market share, and profits in a highly competitive, low-growth market. It's hard to say exactly how much of this was due to the EFQM programme, but this initiative was the primary business performance improvement programme, was sponsored by the CEO, and had the active participation and support of senior leaders. Several leaders cascaded it down their organisation, asking different functions to carry out a similar exercise. Furthermore, the initiative strengthened the hand of those pushing the *Systematic Productivity* culture: it was clear senior executives wanted improvement, and the framework provided a common language for such discussions.

Developmental theory predicts that an initiative like this one offers a powerful lever for change:

- It stimulates transformation to a later action-logic by directly introducing new types of conversation into the group.
- It allows the active participation of senior leaders, who become personal advocates based on their own experiences of the programme, and therefore role-models to the rest of the organisation.
- It empowers people by giving them a framework and tools to think for themselves, and use their own ingenuity.
- It has a competitive element and a fun element.
- It's a long-term initiative that can build up gradually over many years to be become part of Organisation A's culture.

Organisation B is a medium-sized business. It was under-performing financially and brought in a new CEO to turn around the company. The CEO introduced several change initiatives. The immediate need was to cut costs, then to improve efficiency and effectiveness, and eventually to start growing. One change initiative was the introduction of what the CEO calls "Tea and bacon roll meetings." These are roundtables of different groups of employees. The company provides cups of tea and bacon rolls. Employees are asked to bring along a story of a recent success, a question for the CEO, and either a challenge they are facing or an idea for improvement.

The sessions take place every two weeks, each aiming for about eight attendees from a mixture of departments. Each employee will normally attend at least one session a year. In the words of the CEO:

"I've been running these for many years at several companies. The main purposes are: to promote a culture of openness; to give me a chance to understand what is really going on in the business; to provide a forum for people to put forward ideas for improvement; to enable people to ask me questions; and to give people a chance to hear perspectives from people in other teams.

"We get lots of great ideas, and each time I increase my understanding of the business. The best conversations are those that flow quite freely and help people understand the perspective of others in the business. For example, people from sales and operations – who often have very different perspectives – might get into a conversation about a problem, and I can just sit back and listen for 20 minutes.

"The first few times I run it in a company people can be terrified and clammed up. On these occasions, or when the group is reserved, I will put in place a bit of structure by going around the table asking each person in turn to talk through their success, idea or challenge, and question for me. I've also learned that at the beginning it is good to have some talkative people in the group to get things going.

"I tell people they can raise or ask anything. Sometimes people need to get things out of their system, or have had frustrations for many years, but no outlet. On occasions people can be very tense when speaking and won't always speak calmly or articulately. Sometimes it can feel like I'm being attacked verbally. I've learned I need to manage my own emotions. I've noticed that if I react to the emotion or get defensive it closes down the immediate discussion and the rest of the session.

"There have been times the meeting dynamic has been quite negative and I've faced what can seem like a wall of moaning. Here I try to pin people down on specifics, asking exactly what they mean or to give an example. If people respond with more vague complaints, I press them on which is the most important one for them, the one they would most like me to work on.

"It is demanding, it's putting yourself out there to be questioned on anything – and you won't always know whether it will be a quiet session that needs encouragement or a heated discussion. I need to know my subject matter, and I need a flexibility of style. I have encouraged people in my senior team to do this with varying success."

These sessions promote or reinforce several organisational action-logics. They reinforce *Level Four (Experiments)* by requiring each employee to bring along either a challenge for discussion or an idea for improvement. They promote a *Level Five (Systematic Productivity)* awareness by making space for discussions between functions, for example the 20-minute conversation between operations and sales.

In many organisations, such roundtables can be excruciating affairs, a mix of polite formality, awkwardness, and grandstanding. Organisation B's work because of several behaviours by the CEO. If someone is angry or upset, the CEO lets them have their say, and get the emotion out of their system. Faced with lots of negativity or moaning, the CEO balances allowing this to be expressed, with making people work, for example to provide specific examples or identify their top priority for change. The CEO has learned from experience that he can't react to the emotion or get defensive, and that he needs to manage his own emotions.

As people see for themselves how the CEO handles situations like these, and hear about it from their colleagues, people feel more comfortable raising topics that have been bothering them, challenging existing thinking, and asking questions they feel awkward about. All this promotes a culture of openness, higher levels of trust, and illustrates several characteristics of *Level Seven* (*Collaborative Inquiry*).

Organisation B moved from loss to profit within 18 months of the CEO joining, and grew its profits in each of following years. In the first four years of the CEO's tenure, its share price rose 400%.

Developmental theory predicts good prospects for a change initiative like this one: it directly stimulates new types of conversation; it has active participation and role-modelling by senior leaders, in this case the CEO; it has a long-term nature, so the effects build up gradually over many years to become part of Organisation B's culture.

This story also illustrates some of the emotional competencies – empathy, self-awareness, self-regulation – that leaders will need to draw on if their organisation embarks on a journey to *Level Seven*. In such organisations, all voices are heard, and conflict and disagreements are surfaced openly. Organisation B's CEO describes vividly what this can feel like in practice, and it isn't for everybody.

Organisation C is a group of a dozen or so business units, and whose culture was estimated to be spread across *Experiments* and *Systematic Productivity*. Its structure and IT systems, however, were typical of *Experiments*: it was more a federation of independent businesses than a single business itself; each business had a separate IT system, different ways of running their processes, and different definitions for basic performance measures.

In Organisation C, the culture and conversational dynamic was open to discussing the efficiency and effectiveness of the overall whole, but its structure and IT systems made it difficult for these conversations to happen. Organisation C initiated a major IT programme to adopt standard processes on a common IT platform. Once the IT programme was complete – and this took several years – Organisation C changed the structure of the group, in essence merging the 12 business units into a single business with single teams managing integrated functions.

The programme is widely seen as a success. Organisation C outperforms its peers on revenue growth and profit margin in difficult market conditions. In the words of one senior executive, the programme "completely changed how we manage the business."

The lesson from this example is that the culture was ready to move on to a later action-logic, *Systematic Productivity*, but because the IT systems and organisational structure stuck at the characteristic associated with *Experiments*, these conversations couldn't meaningfully take place. The change programme worked because it allowed IT infrastructure and organisational structure to "catch-up" with culture, and enable the whole group to evolve more completely to *Systematic Productivity*.

Organisation D is a group of several business units, whose culture was estimated as spread across *Experiments* and *Systematic Productivity*. It was underperforming financially. The leadership team launched several short-term cost-cutting initiatives, which achieved their targets. The leadership team also identified several operational problems, which arose from the nature of the group's structure – the structure was largely typical of those associated with *Experiments*.

It initiated several waves of organisational change – some large and affecting the whole group, others medium-sized or small affecting particular functions or geographies. Most of these organisational changes were consistent with a move from structures typical of *Experiments* to structures typical of *Systematic Productivity*.

There was no organisation-wide initiative aimed at changing the culture or stimulating new kinds of conversations. The President of one division established his own initiative aimed at cultural change, but it addressed things like "having a can-do attitude" and "setting stretch goals" rather than directly stimulating new types of conversation. What's more, it was launched through the promotional efforts of HR rather than the direct participation and role-modelling of senior leaders. As a result, according to one observer, it had no visible support from any senior leader other than the divisional President, and no visible impact on the workforce. It was quietly dropped the moment the divisional President moved to a different role.

None of the waves of change initiated in Organisation D delivered the performance improvements sought by the management team. The group continued to underperform financially. The changes might have fixed one set of operational problems arising from the previous structure, but a new set of operational problems always emerged from the new structure.

The least effective change was a radical and discontinuous jump in one division from an *Experiments* to a *Systematic Productivity* structure. The culture might have been enough to carry it through, but the IT system wasn't. The

IT system was stuck at *Experiments*, and leaders in the new *Systematic Productivity* organisation did not have the information they needed to do their jobs. Costs spiralled and this major strategic programme was rolled back significantly.

Developmental theory predicts that changing an organisation's structure is unlikely to deliver lasting performance improvement unless it also stimulates or enables a move to a later organisational action-logic. Organisation C achieved this because the changes allowed IT and structure to "catch up" with culture. Organisation D's situation is complex, with likely many factors at play, but the observer attributed its failure to factors such as the following:

- There was no organisation-wide initiative that stimulated new types of conversation.
- The cultural change initiative in one division relied on promotion by HR rather than active participation and role-modelling by senior leaders.
- The leaders perceived the root causes of the operational problems as stemming from the organisational structure. Each time they changed the structure, new operational problems emerged stemming from the new structure.
- Perhaps the real underlying cause was a strong and particular streak of *Experiments* culture that prevented the management ranks from having conversations about the efficiency and effectiveness of the overall whole, and collaborating across divisions to make the whole work.

Large organisations at levels four and five

This section examines issues specific to large organisations transforming from *Level Four* (*Experiments*) to *Level Five* (*Systematic Productivity*). It can be skipped without any loss of flow.

Large organisations have an overall action-logic determined by the overall design of the organisation, but different parts of the organisation could be operating at different levels. Consider a group with ten subsidiaries that operate largely independently. The structure of the overall group is *Level Four* (*Experiments*) because there is no common approach, no shared systems or learning between the subsidiaries. But each subsidiary might be operating at any level, as indeed might different functions within a subsidiary. One subsidiary might have manufacturing at *Five* (*Systematic Productivity*), sales at *Four* (*Experiments*) and Human Resources at *Three* (*Incorporation*).

This paper offers the following conjectures (based on anecdotal information):

- If you could do snapshot of multi-nationals in Europe in the mid-

nineties, a good 80-90% of them would have a dominant organisational action-logic at *Level Four (Experiments)*.

- Nearly all corporate transformation efforts over the last 20 years can
  be seen through a lens of either transforming from *Four (Experiments)*
  to *Five (Systematic Productivity)* or strengthening the *Systematic Productivity* action-logic.

- Large businesses that are near completion of this transformation are
  probably leaders in their sector. The majority of large businesses are
  probably still in this transformation, and there are likely some who
  haven't started or have barely started.

Several factors have contributed to this (conjectured) historical dominance of *Experiments*. Most large multinationals in Europe grew by merger
and acquisition, and this introduced an inevitable *Experiments* structure as the
acquired companies have their own processes, IT systems, and culture. The
limitations of IT and telecoms infrastructure – as will be seen in a moment –
made it difficult for a large, geographically diverse organisation to evolve to
Systematic Productivity. Furthermore, research (see *Action Inquiry* Chapter 5)
shows that only a minority of managers have reached the corresponding
Achiever individual action-logic needed to lead at *Systematic Productivity*.

At least four major trends fuelled the transformation of large businesses
to *Systematic Productivity* over the last two decades. First, consultants such as
McKinsey & Company identified, analysed, quantified, and promoted the
benefits of moving from *Experiments* to *Systematic Productivity* (although they
didn't use this language). Consider, by way of example, a multi-national insurance company that grew over the years by merger and acquisition and has,
say, around 60 independent business units. These 60 business units would all
have had their own approach, processes and IT systems for assessing risk,
pricing policies, and managing claims. The consultancy firm would analyse
this situation and propose to top management that, say, 55 of those business
units should have the same process for pricing policies and managing claims,
and adopt a common IT system to manage it all. And that the group should
create integrated pricing and claims functions to manage these activities
across the organisation. The consultants might also show that if the current
state costs, say, three billion dollars a year, the future state would cost only
two billion. All this represents a transformation to *Systematic Productivity*.

Second, more powerful technology makes it considerably easier to move
to common IT systems, and hence common processes and a shared approach. In the insurance example above, twenty years ago it would have been
prohibitively expensive and high risk to try to integrate claims processing
across 55 business units. Now this is possible, and businesses such as SAP,
Oracle, IBM, Capgemini, and Accenture do a lot of business making it happen.

Third is the growth of outsourcing, which offers a relatively quick way to transform a function from *Experiments* to *Systematic Productivity*. Suppose an organisation has 20,000 employees across 20 business units, and all these employees need their own phone, laptop, software and IT support. If each business unit were managing this independently, the IT support function would be operating overall at *Experiments*. An easy way to move to *Systematic Productivity* would be ask an IT outsourcing provider to manage it all as an integrated, single service. Such outsourcing deals typically specify detailed Service Level Agreements (SLAs) and require year-on-year improvement to ensure the outsourcing provider operates at *Systematic Productivity*. Outsourcing is also transforming other functions such as payroll and benefits, HR support, invoice processing, and customer service.

Fourth is growth in consultancy firms that help businesses embed change and continual improvement in their day-to-day operational processes, and the wide range of tools available – egg, Six Sigma, ISO9001, Agile Management, Balanced Scorecards – to support such a transformation.

Summary

One key theme of this work is the difference between the conversational dynamics of a stage (its ability to have different kinds of conversations), and organisational characteristics such as structure and processes. Table 4.1 summarises these. Note that the conversational ability of a stage includes all the conversational abilities of earlier stages. At *Systematic Productivity*, for example, an organisation is still able to discuss the new ideas of *Experiments*; and at *Social network*, an organisation retains the ability to discuss *Systematic Productivity's* effectiveness of the whole. The organisational characteristics – structures, processes etc. – are not necessarily carried forward.

A second key theme is that imposing a structure or process of a later-stage on organisation with earlier-stage conversation dynamics causes dysfunction. Chapter 2 described how the cafe manager was stuck with an unsuitable coffee brand because the central purchasing function could not listen and discuss feedback; the business unit leaders had problems with HR or IT support that they couldn't fix, and the central HR or IT support teams won't listen to or discuss feedback. Likewise imposing Laloux's Teal practices such as self-organising teams or complete information transparency on an organisation that does not have the openness and trust to have the required conversations is likely to cause dysfunction.

Table 4.1: Summary of defining and associated characteristics by stage

	Conversational abilities	Typical structures, processes, etc.
Three (Incorporation)	Not able or willing to discuss new ideas, changes to the work done, or how it is carried out.	Might have a simple structure, or could be a division or function in a larger organisation.
Four (Experiments)	Able to discuss new ideas, and starting new activities. Starting new activities is easier to discuss openly than stopping existing ones.	Silos, fragmentation, complexity, being spread too thinly.
Five (Systematic Productivity)	Able to discuss the efficiency and effectiveness of the overall whole based on an understanding of cause and effect. Equally at ease openly discussing starting and stopping activities.	Standardisation, shared services (e.g., common HR or IT functions serving multiple business units), prevalence of measures and targets.
Six (Social Network)	Able to question underlying assumptions and mindsets, and explore alternatives.	Autonomous, non-hierarchical units connected by shared vision and collaboration.
Seven (Collaborative Inquiry)	Shared reflection on vision... open rather than masked interpersonal relations... multiple kinds of feedback... paradoxes to be explored... discussion of structures appropriate to the moment.	The Teal practices described in *Reinventing Organisations,* such as self-management, information transparency, and elimination of staff functions.

* In part three, these characteristics are treated a little differently, as separate *conversational* and *organisational action-logics*.

Part one of this work aimed to help people understand the different kinds of conversations that can take place, and their implications for the organisation. Part two turns to how to use the model in practice.

Primer

PART TWO

FIELD MANUAL

FIVE

Tools to work with the framework

Anyone wanting to work with the framework will need to get others interested in it and its potential to help them achieve their goals. The following five pages (starting "An Executive Summary for Organisational Leaders" and ending with "Table 5.2: organisational operating systems and upgrades") aim to do this. It can be used as:

- An easy-to-digest overview of the framework.
- A brochure for consultants and coaches to send to their clients.
- A sales tool that consultants can use in meetings with potential clients.
- A self-assessment tool.
- Pre-read for a workshop, with tables 5.1 and 5.2 used for group discussion in the workshop.

Table 5.2 itself can be used as a one-page summary of the model. It is intended to be easy to absorb and discuss. The columns – success measures, change initiatives, and conversations about change – were chosen because they provide good clues to an organisation's level, are tangible, and easy to picture and investigate. The bottom row is *Level Three* (*Incorporation*), which then rises through *Experiments*, *Systematic Productivity*, *Social Network*, and *Collaborative Inquiry*. It's laid out vertically, partly because the phrase "vertical development" is sometimes used to describe transformation from one action-logic to the next, but also to avoid comparisons with a capability- or process-maturity matrix.

Table 5.3 on the subsequent page is more abstract, emphasising the relationship between conversations and organisational characteristics. This table is intended for people who want further information, or who are already familiar with developmental theory.

Parts of Chapter 5 are open source. This means people have full permission to: use them, take the bits they want, rework and rephrase them, change the formatting, adapt to fit with other tools and terminologies, and so on. The open source parts are:

- The Executive Summary in next five pages (starting "An Executive Summary for Organisational Leaders" and ending with "Table 5.2: organisational operating systems and upgrades").
- Table 5.1: Self-assessment questionnaire for prevalence of different kinds of conversation
- Table 5.2: organisational operating systems and upgrades
- Table 5.3: How conversations shape organisations
- Table 5.4: Checklist of capabilities or lessons to learn by level
- Table 5.5: Lagging and leading aspects
- Table 5.6: Double-loop learning tool
- Table 5.7: Example of double-loop learning

The latest open-source tools can be downloaded at tiny.cc/gah96y. If this link doesn't work, please email ianharcus3@gmail.com.

An executive summary for organisational leaders

Organisational change initiatives have a notoriously poor track record. A McKinsey & Company article, *Transformation with a Capital T* (2016), states "the reported failure rate of large-scale change programs has hovered around 70 percent over many years." The authors go on to wonder "How many times have frontline managers told us things like 'we have undergone three transformations in the last eight years, and each time we were back where we started 18 months later'?"

This Executive Summary introduces a different way to think about organisational performance and change. It identifies clear reasons why change initiatives fail so regularly, and offers a different approach to improve chances of success. It also aims to be practical: to help people in organisations find steps they can take to make their group more effective, responsive, and enjoyable.

The heart of the model refers to the kinds of conversations that take place in an organisation. For example, one group may find it hard to discuss new ideas; another may find it easy to discuss starting new activities, but harder to discuss stopping existing ones; a third may be at ease exploring underlying assumptions and goals.

The model claims that dynamics such as these are pivotal to any group's success. It proposes a series of developmental stages for these dynamics, where organisations moving to later stages acquire greater agility, resilience, and effectiveness by being able to have different kinds of conversations – a bit like an organisational operating system upgrade.

This has many implications for organisations: how to deliver lasting performance improvements; how to avoid wasting money on change programmes that don't deliver; how to get a visible return from leadership development and coaching. But first an overview of the model…

Imagine working at the following four organisations.

The first is established, profitable, and stable, but perhaps a little stuck in its ways. You spot a few things that might be done a little better, and eventually make a gentle suggestion. You get an abrupt response: "that's not how we do things around here." A few weeks later in a friendly, informal meeting, you make another gentle suggestion. There's an awkward silence for a moment, and then someone changes the subject. You privately sound out a colleague, who says it's best when people just get on with their job and don't make waves.

At the second organisation, people are always making suggestions. If there's one thing that's guaranteed to get folks excited, it's exploring a new idea. There are lots of projects, lots of new initiatives. After a while you realise this organisation never has any conversations about how well these initiatives fit together, or how well the organisation works as a whole. It finds it difficult to stop a project, or to focus on a smaller number of initiatives. As a result, it has too many activities going on, which don't always contribute much. In this organisation, the whole is less than the sum of the parts.

At the third, there are also conversations about new ideas, but with greater discipline. This organisation has a clearly defined purpose and high-level goals, plenty of targets and success measures, and it evaluates new ideas against all these. It also discusses the overall portfolio of initiatives, and how well the organisation works as a whole. As a result, it focuses on a smaller number of initiatives that really make a difference, and finds it easy to discuss stopping activities. This organisation performs well. Yet it finds it harder to discuss things that aren't covered by its targets and measures, such as what really matters to them and their stakeholders as individuals, or whether their targets and measures have any negative consequences. It can be a bit of a performance machine, overlooking the human side. It has blind spots.

The fourth organisation is a bit harder to describe. Your new colleagues routinely explore the relevance of different goals, and seek to surface assumptions about different approaches. As a result they get to the heart of what really matters more often. They tolerate radically different mindsets and approaches across the organisation, and this makes them innovative and inventive. People also discuss what really matters to them as individuals, what kind of world they want to live in, and their implications for how the organisation should operate. They balance efficiency and humanity better than the previous organisations.

Readers are invited to consider which of the above dynamics they recognise, and where their current organisation might be. The first table below is a self-assessment grid to help with this, and could usefully be carried out by an entire team. (An organisation here can be a team, department, division, company or non-profit, so a finance department might consider itself both as an independent organisation and as part of a larger whole.)

One implication of the model is that an organisation that never has conversations about how well it works as whole is unlikely to work well as a whole.

A second is that introducing such conversations will likely lead to many new initiatives to get the organisation working well as a whole. The organisation changes as its operating system upgrades take hold. The second table below describes how organisations at different stages measure performance, and the natures the changes within them – there will be other changes too, for example to structure, processes and IT systems. Readers are also invited to use this table as an organisational self-assessment tool.

A third implication is that conventional approaches to change won't work. These tend to involve designing a new operating model, implementing it, and expecting lasting performance improvement. These seldom work, partly because no design will ever be perfect, but also because if you want your organisation to work well as a whole, you need to find ways of making the required conversations part of the culture. Conventional approaches to change overlook this.

The model was developed by Bill Torbert in the late eighties. The four organisations described above are respectively at the stages called *Incorporation*, *Experiments*, *Systematic Productivity* and *Social Network*. There's work ongoing to create practical tools to help people apply the theory.

Pick a unit – perhaps your team, department, immediate organisation, or wider organisation – and think about the kinds of conversations that take place, and how easy they are to have. For each type of conversation tick the box that most closely corresponds to the frequency and ease of the conversation.

Table 5.1: Self-assessment questionnaire for prevalence of different kins of conversation

Conversations about…	Don' t really happen in our team / organisation	Happen occasionally, perhaps in private, and can be awkward or unfamiliar	Are common enough, but not habitual	Are part of our culture
Starting something new, or doing something differently (*Experiments stage*)				
Stopping or discontinuing an existing project or activity (*Systematic Productivity stage*)				
How well our team or organisation works as a whole. Whether the whole is greater than the sum of the parts. (*Systematic Productivity stage*)				
What really matters in a given situation? What is it behind a goal or target that really matters? What is " success beyond the numbers" ? (*Social Network stage*)				

Table 5.2: Organisational "operating systems and upgrades" (start at the bottom row and work up)

	Success measures	Change initiatives	Conversations about change
Collaborative Inquiry	"All information available in real time to all, including about company financials and compensation."*	Initiatives "emerge organically from the collective intelligence of self-managing employees."*	Shared reflection on vision... open rather than masked interpersonal relations... multiple kinds of feedback... paradoxes to be explored... discussion of structures appropriate to the moment.
Social Network	We pay attention to how the precise definitions of measures influence people's behaviours, either positively or negatively. We also consider aspects of success we can't usefully measure (success beyond the numbers).	We have a diverse set of inventive change initiatives at grassroots level. Our structure and processes make it hard for the centre to veto a committed local team.	We inquire into the relevance of different goals, seek to surface assumptions, and tolerate radically different views. From time to time we stumble across breakthrough solutions emerging from unexpected and completely new angles.
Systematic Productivity	We invest time and money to measure what is important and useful. We track both the outcomes that matter, as well as the operational causes or enablers that drive them.	We focus on the results our change initiatives achieve. We concentrate our efforts on a smaller number of initiatives, and follow through to ensure they make a difference to results.	Our focus on top-level goals makes it equally easy to discuss starting new activities and stopping existing ones. We discuss how well the different parts of the organisation work together.
Experiments	We have lots of measures. There are some important things we should track better than we do, and others we monitor because they're easy to measure, rather than because they drive much useful discussion.	We have lots of change initiatives, perhaps too many. We don't always know what impact they have on our high-level goals, e.g., financial results.	We find it easy to discuss starting new projects and activities. We find it harder to discuss stopping existing ones.
Incorp.	We measure what we're required to, such as financials.	There's little change in our organisation, unless mandated by external factors, e.g., orders from on high or regulations.	Discussing doing things differently makes people uncomfortable...

*Reinventing Organisations, Frederic Laloux

46

Table 5.3: How conversations shape organisations (start at the bottom row and work up)

	Conversational capacity	Typical structures, processes	Strengths and limitations
Collaborative Inquiry	Shared reflection on vision... open rather than masked interpersonal relations... multiple kinds of feedback... paradoxes to be explored... discussion of structures appropriate to the moment.	"Self-organising teams... [elimination of staff functions so] most such functions performed by teams themselves... peer-based processes for individual performance."*	Agile, high-performing, fulfilling, "unleash[ing] unprecedented energy and creativity."*
Social Network	Inquiry into the relevance of different goals, questioning underlying assumptions and mindsets, toleration of different approaches.	Autonomous, non-hierarchical units connected by shared vision and collaboration.	Being able to address both efficiency and the human element. Being the voice of humanity and individuality. Relies on strength of shared vision and mission to hold together.
Systematic Productivity	Equally easy to discuss starting new activities and stopping existing ones. Regular conversations about how well the different parts of the organisation work together, and the causes and effects of overall performance.	Standardisation, shared services (e.g., common HR or IT functions serving multiple business units), prevalence of measures and targets.	High performing organisation. Risk of over-standardisation, over-looking the human element, undesirable side effects of measurement and target setting.
Experiments	Able to discuss new ideas and starting new activities. Harder to discuss stopping existing ones.	Lots of innovation initiatives and activities. Decentralised, autonomous business unit structure.	Being able to improve, innovate and evolve. Risk of silos, fragmentation, complexity, being spread too thinly – the whole is less than the sum of the parts.
Incorp.	Unable or unwilling to discuss new ideas or doing things differently.	Might have a simple structure, or could be a division or function in a larger organisation.	Achieving viability and stability. Honouring heritage or tradition. Limited ability to react to external change.

*Reinventing Organisations, Frederic Laloux

Putting the framework into practice

Long involved discussions about which level an organisation is at are not recommended, particularly when first working with the framework. A three-hour workshop with a senior team should be ample to cover explaining the framework, reaching a "good enough" approximation of where the organisation is at present, a discussion where it wants to be, and to at least start discussions of things they might try differently. Support from someone familiar with the theory and able to check and challenge participants is highly recommended.

There are several reasons to avoid trying to be too scientific about where an organisation is. First, the power of the framework is best discovered by putting into practice some of its insights and recommendations and seeing what happens. For example, an organisation might, during its annual planning process, ask each function to: a) explicitly consider which activities it should scale back or stop all together so they can focus on higher priorities; and b) consider how well they think the organisation works together, and which other functions they might work better with. Actions like these will allow people to see the possibilities of the framework and decide whether they find this way of thinking useful.

Second is the discussions could get complicated quickly, as most organisations will be spread across more than one level. In one business familiar to the author, *Experiments* conversations are fully embedded in the culture. *Systematic Productivity* conversations happen and are widely accepted, but don't happen as often as they should. *Social Network* conversations do take place to a small degree – and have been consciously promoted – but are still unfamiliar in the business. This organisation's centre of gravity is at *Systematic Productivity*, though it still has a trailing edge at *Experiments*, and an emergent leading edge at *Social Network*. (Chapter 4 gives other examples of organisations spread across more than one level.)

The core tools for assessment are tables 5.1 and 5.2 above. Table 5.2 is based on the following the three questions below, which get to the heart of the kinds of conversations that take place in an organisation, and how it learns and responds to change. (Further detail on these is in chapters 2 and 3).

- How do you measure success?
- How has what you do – e.g., products, services, activities – changed in recent years?
- How do you manage the organisation's performance? Assuming it involves meetings, what happens in those meetings?

Once a team or organisation has assessed where their centre of gravity is – again, ideally with support from someone familiar with the theory and able to check and challenge them – the next step is to discuss what they want to do. They might decide they wish to reinforce some kinds of existing conversations, staying at the same stage, but solidifying it. And they may decide they wish to introduce new kinds of conversations, seeking to transform to the next stage

Tables 5.4 and 5.5 are designed to help with this. Using Table 5.4, for example, an organisation might conclude it checks all the boxes for *Incorporation* and *Experiments*, but has more lessons to learn from *Systematic Productivity*. That guides what it might do next.

Table 5.4: Checklist of capabilities or lessons to learn by level

Incorporation	• Honours social norms and traditions that have value.
	• Has stable and cordial relations with outside parties.
Experiments	• People propose, explore and implement new ideas without defensiveness or awkwardness. New ideas and doing things differently are part of the culture.
Systematic productivity	• Knows both what success looks like, and the operational enablers (causes) of success.
	• Able to both start and stop activities. Avoids too many activities.
	• Gathers feedback, e.g. customer and employee satisfaction.
	• Reflecting on performance, lessons learned and what can be improved is part of the culture.
	• The parts of the organisation work together well so the whole is at least the sum of the parts.
Social network	• Challenges goals, asks what really matters, considers success beyond the numbers.
	• Tries out radically different approaches, embraces radically different mindsets.

Table 5.5 aims to help people discuss what might be holding them back, and therefore identify what kind of change initiatives might help them most. For example, an HR function in a large organisation seeking to establish itself at *Systematic Productivity* might identify that HR teams in different divisions have success measures with different definitions, so they can't compare team performance.

Table 5.6 is designed to help organisations experiment with double-loop learning. It is recommended particularly for *Systematic Productivity* and *Social Network* organisations, and best avoided in *Incorporation* organisations.

Table 5.5: Lagging and leading aspects

Relative to centre of gravity...	Lags	Supports	Leads
Organisational structure			
IT infrastructure			
Management reporting, key performance indicators			
Management processes, including governance, approvals, key meetings			
Explicit, 'official' values			
Unwritten rules and norms			
Senior leader archetype: what's the mould for the kind of people who reach senior ranks?			
Other			

Most goals – for example, "win the war drugs" – have assumptions and a strategy embedded within them. Points 1-4 of the double-loop learning tool aim to separate the assumptions and strategy from the goal. For example, compare points 2 & 4 in Table 5.7: point 2 is a goal with embedded assumptions and strategy; point 4 is a more open goal that gets to the root of what really matters.

Point 5, bringing in different thinking is important because it is entirely natural and human for people to get attached to and identify with a particular strategy. Bringing in different people to suggest ideas is a good way around this. Likewise point 7 is hugely important: if there is no regret or pain, then it probably wasn't double-loop learning, and the proposed solution may have excluded more radical possibilities.

Table 5.6: Double-loop learning tool

1. Describe a problem, perhaps where the organisation is fighting a losing battle.

2. Pinpoint the current goal

3. Why does the goal matter? Describe the underlying factors that make this goal important.

4. Try rephrasing the goal, removing any reference to the original goal, instead rephrasing it solely in terms of the underlying factors that really matter.

5. How can you now bring in some different thinking?

6. [To be filled in later] Proposed new approach

7. [To be filled in later] Be open about the pain and regret

Table 5.7: Example of double-loop learning

1. Describe a problem, perhaps where the organisation is fighting a losing battle.

London Underground (LU) had a problem with buskers – musicians who performed without authorisation and solicited money from passengers.

LU tried to eradicate buskers, as they were a nuisance and safety risk. Police would caution them and arrest persistent offenders. LU itself would put up posters and make loudspeaker announcements asking passengers not to give them any money.

None of this worked; the buskers remained; it was a losing battle.

2. Pinpoint the current goal

Eradicate buskers

3. Why does the goal matter? Describe the underlying factors that make this goal important.

They are a safety risk as they cause crowd bottlenecks.

They damage passenger experience as the quality of their music is variable and they can be aggressive in asking for money.

4. Try rephrasing the goal, removing any reference to the original goal, instead rephrasing it solely in terms of the underlying factors that really matter.

One possibility is, "how can London underground ensure the persistence of buskers does not create any safety risk or damage passenger experience?"

5. How can you now bring in some different thinking?

Perhaps they might discuss the rephrased goal with a group of teenagers, college students, customers, suppliers, or job applicants.

6. [To be filled in later] Proposed new approach

Maybe it was a process like this that led to the launch in 2003 of the LU Busking Scheme. This scheme does not see buskers as a nuisance and does not try to eradicate them; instead it welcomes them, and uses other approaches to address the safety and passenger experience problems. The LU Busking Scheme provides approved busker zones (solving the safety & bottleneck problem), an audition and licensing process and a code of conduct (solving the customer experience problem). It's funded by advertising and sponsorship. As the LU website puts it, "The London Underground (LU) Busking Scheme is a hit with performers and the traveling public. Passengers enjoy more than 100,000 hours of live music performed every year by professional, talented buskers."

7. [To be filled in later] Be open about the pain and regret

To the people involved in the original strategy – those who cautioned buskers, arrested them, made loudspeaker announcements asking passengers not to give them any money, or set and measured targets for getting rid of them – this new strategy may seem like a defeat, like giving in. It's a legitimate view, and one that would naturally come with feelings of pain and regret. It's worth making the space to explicitly acknowledge and mourn the abandonment of the previous strategy and identity.

SIX

Possible strategies for change

This chapter suggests some possible strategies for transforming from one action-logic to the next. These suggestions come with the following caveats:

- Transforming from one level to the next is a culture change, and cultural change takes time. The tables suggest new behaviours, and leaders might need to put conscious effort into these new behaviours for many years before they become a new "habit" for the organisation.
- The behaviour of an organisation's leaders sets the tone for the organisation. To transform to the next level, role-modelling by senior leaders is vital.
- External help or support is likely to be needed, particularly for the organisation's leaders.

Any or all of the sections in this chapter can be skipped – they may be more useful as reference material, rather than to read straight through.

A possible strategy for transforming from
Incorporation to *Experiments*

At *Incorporation*, people are uncomfortable proposing, receiving, evaluating, and discussing new ideas. Transformation to *Experiments* involves introducing such conversations. The challenge is that at *Incorporation*, people attach great importance to being polite, saving face, and not causing any unpleasantness. Making suggestions for doing things differently risks loss of face for both the proposer and the recipient.

The approach suggested here is to try to introduce new social norms that make it less risky for people to suggest, receive and try out new ideas. The elements of this are: train and coach leaders how to evaluate, respond to, and encourage new ideas; promote new explicit social norms for making suggestions in a polite and considerate way; finding ways to try new ideas.

Training and coaching leaders how to evaluate, respond to, and encourage new ideas might include:

- Frameworks for evaluating new ideas, and meetings to review several ideas at a time.
- Learning to give an idea time. If the initial instinct is to reject it for some reason, practice responding by inquiring into the thinking behind it, e.g., "talk me through how that might work in practice" or with remarks like "Thank you for that idea, let me mull it over.
- Establishing a safety net for people whose ideas get shot down, e.g., saying in public "well that was a great conversation. It looks like we won't be moving forward with the idea, but I'm glad we discussed it – thank you, Sam, for raising it" and in private, coach them on how they might test ideas beforehand (see below).
- Using external events and what-if questions to trigger conversations, e.g. "I see our competitor has just launched a new website. How about [conspiratorial look] we take a look to see if we should copy any of their ideas?" or "The business we get from the internet is already 25% of sales, and someone was telling me that will go up to 50%. What if it were to become 50% of our business, what would we need to do differently?"
- Regularly asking for ideas and suggestions, e.g., "if anybody's got any suggestions on how we can improve, come and see me for a chat, or drop me an email". Persist over many months, even if the initial suggestions don't elicit a response.
- Planting suggestions in meetings, e.g., when someone makes a good point in private, rather than approve it straight away, express general support and ask them to raise it at the next team meeting, perhaps testing it with a few others first. The aim of this is to introduce and reinforce the practice or proposing and discussing ideas in meetings.

Promoting new explicit social norms for making suggestions in a polite and considerate way might include

- Linking it to something external (as above) so it doesn't imply any criticism; testing it first in private with someone, giving them time to mull it over; then testing it with others, giving themselves time to mull over any feedback.
- Codifying aspects of the above, or something similar, into a set of public rules for polite and considerate idea sharing.

Finding ways to try new ideas could involve minimising risk through small-scale trials, e.g., one time with one customer.

A possible strategy for transforming from *Experiments* to *Systematic Productivity*

At *Experiments*, the different parts of an organisation may be reasonably well optimised, but optimised in isolation. The transformation to *Systematic Productivity* involves introducing conversations about how well the organisation works as a whole.

Such conversations directly threaten the autonomy of the parts, whether those parts are different subsidiaries, functions, or local teams. The benefits of autonomy at *Experiments* include accountability and job satisfaction: those managing a part are generally empowered to make decisions and can see the consequences. The transformation to *Systematic Productivity* tends to limit these, so new sources of accountability and job satisfaction will need be found.

Autonomy also provides a conflict-management mechanism (of sorts). *Experiments* organisations may have an unwritten rule that the different parts "mind their own business." Such an unwritten rule allows conflict to be managed (or at least avoided), but is incompatible with the transformation to *Systematic Productivity*. Therefore, a new approach to conflict management will be needed

A strategy for transformation to *Systematic Productivity* therefore needs to: motivate people to have conversations about how the organisation works as a whole; prompt these to happen regularly; provide new sources of job satisfaction to replace any lost autonomy; and provide new approaches to conflict management to replace any unwritten "mind our own business" or similar rule.

The strategy suggested here is to implement a systematic approach to *measurement*. If job satisfaction at *Experiments* comes from autonomy and accountability, at *Systematic Productivity*, it is more likely to come from working together to deliver the outcomes that matter, and seeing the impact of one's efforts on overall performance. Likewise, high-level outcomes provide a new source of conflict management. The elements of this are: define high-level outcomes and operational enablers; adopt a process approach to change; and create learning loops

Defining high-level outcomes and operational enablers might include:

- Defining – perhaps with the help of external consultants / specialists – the important outcomes for the business/department/team to deliver, what measures should be in place to track them and the operational factors (causes) that would create these outcomes (sometimes called *process measures*).
- Spending time and money to put in place measures and reporting for

these outcomes and operational causes.

- Doing this well is vital for the measures to provide new sources of job satisfaction and a means to resolve conflicts. This includes getting the cause-and-effect aspect right – operational causes of customer- and financial-outcomes, and ensuring that high-level outcomes include measures such as customer satisfaction.

Adopting a process approach to change might include:

- Putting in place a process for regularly occurring items, for example quarterly meetings to review all proposals for new products, discuss the overall portfolio of existing products, and consider candidates for products to be dropped.
- Paying greater attention to setting a small number of priorities, and stopping other activities in order to focus on what's really crucial (according to the high-level outcomes and operational enablers above). Practice asking questions such as "would we get better overall results if we focused all our efforts on these top three activities to make sure they really do deliver?" or "that's good project, but does it really contribute enough to our high-level goals?"

Creating learning loops might include introducing formal stages of review and reflection into each process (learning loops) to stimulate continual improvement of that process. In the above example of the quarterly meeting on product launches and product portfolio management, this might involve adding into the agenda: what did we plan to do in the previous quarter? How did we do? What lessons can we learn from the last quarter? What changes, if any, should we make to our process to capture those lessons? what goals and initiatives will we plan for the next quarter? (Processes like these have names such as Plan-Do-Review, Assess-Plan-Do-Review, Plan-Do-Check-Act, and so on.)

A possible strategy for transforming from *Systematic Productivity* to *Social Network*

A *Systematic Productivity* organisation may be reasonably well optimised, with the parts working together effectively to deliver the defined goals of the organisation. The transformation to *Social Network* involves introducing conversations to explore underlying assumptions and mindsets.

There are likely to be several challenges to introducing such conversations. First, most people will be unaware of their assumptions and mindsets, unfamiliar – and possibly uncomfortable – discussing them, and many will challenge the usefulness and value of doing so. Second, the nature of such conversations is they open up new and unexpected possibilities, and this is inherently destabilising and unpredictable. Third, whereas the transformation to *Systematic Productivity* is a well-trodden path in our culture, with an abundance of tools and consultants available to help, the transformation to *Social Network* isn't. There are few reference points, and for most it will be an exploration of new territory. In short, there is much for people to resist.

A strategy for transformation to *Social Network* might therefore: equip people with tools to help them explore their assumptions and mindsets; identify issues where such discussions will be more obviously useful; focus on first steps to try (accepting the exploratory nature of this journey). The elements of the strategy are: identify points of system failure; explore assumptions and mindsets, that is try out double-loop learning; and allow radical experiments.

Identifying points of system failure might involve asking:

- Is the organisation fighting any losing or unwinnable battles?
- What are the implications of the various success measures used. Do any have negative consequences or encourage "gaming the system" behaviour?
- Does the organisation over-specify, over-standardise, or over-measure? Consult front-line employees, team leaders, customers, or other at-the-coalface stakeholders to understand their perspective. Where do they think central specifications, standards, and measures help real success, and where do they hinder real success? What might "success beyond the measures" mean for them?
- Are there groups of stakeholders who are unhappy, dissatisfied, or let down by the organisation?

Exploring assumptions and mindsets / try out double-loop learning might include:

- For some goals – especially those where the organisation may be fighting a losing battle – ask "why does this goal matter? What are the underlying factors that make this goal important?" Try rephrasing the goal to remove any reference to the original success measure, instead phrasing it solely in terms of the underlying factors that really matter. This then becomes the perfect opportunity to bring in some different thinking, e.g., discuss the rephrased goal with a group of teenagers, college students, customers, suppliers, or job applicants. See tables 18 & 19 in section 5 for a tool to do this.
- Experiment with different success measures or different definitions of the measures, paying particular attention to the behaviours they incentivise or disincentivise.
- Practice asking, "what really matters here?" At the deepest level, "what, at heart, matters to us? What is worthy of being our lives' work?"

Allowing radical experiments could involve

- Do any of the above conversations identify parts of the group that are interested in trying out a radically different approach – the kind of approach that might make others in the group recoil with horror? How about creating some kind of organisational island or ring-fence to allow such an experiment to take place?
- In a similar vein, consider letting a team or business unit implement an idea the leadership completely disagree with, especially if the team seems enthusiastic or the problem knotty and intractable. Say something like, "well we think you're nuts but, why not, give it a go. Nothing else anybody's tried has worked and you sure are enthusiastic."
- Experiment with creating team goals, where a team discusses, defines, and decides a goal that they will be jointly accountable for. (See *The Wisdom of Teams* by Katzenbach and Smith.)

A possible strategy for transforming from *Social Network* to *Collaborative Inquiry*

The defining feature of *Social Network* is that different mindsets and approaches flourish because the culture tends to celebrate differentiation rather than conformity (while maintaining some degree of efficiency). This is both its strength (tolerating different mindsets) and its weakness (no mechanism for resolving the different mindsets).

The challenge is to create levels of openness and trust so people feel comfortable voicing deep but possibly uncomfortable thoughts and feelings, suspending judgment and attachment to existing views, safe in the knowledge that all voices will be heard; thereby creating the space to allow new mindsets to emerge, crystallise, and be explored.

Possible ways of tackling this include the following (and Chapters 10 and 11 of *Action Inquiry* describe the journey of one organisation):

- Seek to create new levels of openness and trust. Experiment with disclosing personal weaknesses, failings, doubts, fears, and creating an environment and social norms that make it visibly safe for others to follow if they so wish (but without any pressure to do so).
- Create forums where each voice/opinion is heard and feels it is heard… and is simultaneously both respected and acknowledged, yet challenged with searching questions… to make strategy and intent more visible… and which suspends immediate judgement to allow novel ideas to be raised, explored and incubated. One outcome of such forums should be "creative resolution of paradoxes", i.e., new

approaches that blend the advantages of the existing (but incompatible) mindsets within the *Social Network*.

- An early topic for such a forum is the organisation's mission and how well that mission is supported (or limited) by the current structure and strategy.

- Another topic is how to merge doing and learning (or action and inquiry), creating structures, processes, and mechanisms that provide individuals, teams, and the organisation with multiple types of feedback.

- The Teal practices described in *Reinventing Organisations* will likely provide plenty of further material, but as with any level, it is the conversational dynamics that define it, not any particular concrete day-to-day practice.

SEVEN

A logical sequence of developmental steps

This chapter introduces a different facet of the model, that of a logical and strategic sequence of steps. It works for any kind of initiative, from a project, to a transformational change programme, to creating a new organisation. Table 7.1 summarises the steps.

Figure 7.1

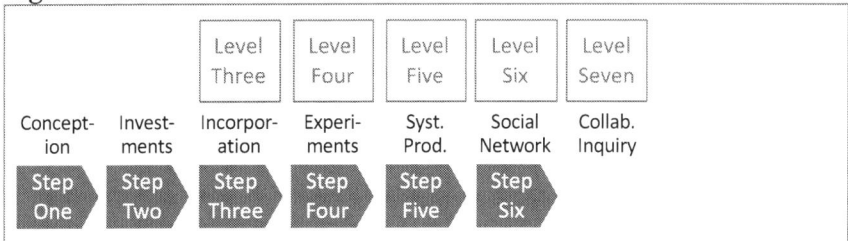

The *Steps* mirror the *Levels* covered in Chapters One to Six. The difference is the *Levels* describe an organisation that has settled stably at a stage, perhaps for many years. With *Steps*, the emphasis is on passing through a stage purposefully on the way to later stages.

Step One (***Conception***) is an idea in people's minds. The advice of the model is: take time to explore and refine the idea before trying to make it happen. In practice, this might mean, when you share the idea with your friend, co-worker, or relative, instead of immediately asking them for help or support, just share the idea, give them a chance to absorb and react to it; listen. You're likely to strengthen your idea, or at least better understand its strengths and weaknesses, and you're allowing time for their enthusiasm to develop before you ask for anything. Or before you go to a bank for a loan, really think through the idea, test it with others, and understand the challenges and risks associated with it. You'll take a better proposal to the bank and be more prepared for the conversation.

In summary, this *Step* is about focus on testing and improving the idea, and restraint from jumping too quickly to implementing it or asking funds.

Table 7.1: A strategic sequence of steps

Step One (Conception)	• Develop the initial concept and vision. Test and refine it so it is sufficiently compelling to succeed at *Step Two*
Step Two (Investments)	• Assemble the resources: people, skills and experience, financial capital, equipment – but also emotional resources such as enthusiasm and commitment – so that it can succeed at *Step Three*.
Step Three (Incorporation)	• Deliver with the resources available, and achieve viability within its context. For a business, this means generating a profit; for a project, showing a return on investment.
Step Four (Experiments)	• "Truly experiment" to find "a viable combination of strategy and structure that can be systematised" at *Step Five*. (*Managing the Corporate Dream* p71)
Step Five (Systematic Productivity)	• Systematise and formalise the organisation, in a way such that the parts of the organisation work together well as a whole and continually improve.
Step Six (Social Network)	• Introduce non-hierarchical ways of working, creating space for different mindsets and counter-cultural approaches to be tried out.

Step Two (Investments) is about finding the resources and investments needed to make the idea a reality. Torbert's writings emphasise two kinds of investment: the emotional investment of the founders, and their ability to get support from other people. In *Managing the Corporate Dream*, he writes:

"The primary investment necessary to give a new organisation a fighting chance is… the commitment of those starting it to its vision and to the work of making it come true… The second most important investment necessary is the investment by a peer network in the nascent organisation…

"One entrepreneur launched his new business by writing to 200 former colleagues or clients, asking them for advice*, money or other resources, if they thought the proposal viable and worthy. Four warned against moving forward. In so doing*, they alerted the entrepreneur to dangers and difficulties he might otherwise have underestimated until it was too late. Another 76 provided a wide range of more positive support, advice, access to resources at cost, free space for the start-up period, and some $10,000 of financing in the form of gifts." (pages 21-23)

*These aspects revisit *Conception*.

Money is also important. If your internet start-up has $1m funding and your competitor up the road has $50m, you are likely to lose. Your competitor will be able to afford more and better developers, more and better sales people, and will likely be able to launch a product with more features, quicker, and with a bigger splash in the market. However, Torbert points out that if you have committed founders supported by a strong peer network, you are more likely to get the resources you need. If you have money but neither of these, you are heading towards an "undistinguished" organisation.

In summary, this stage is about focus on getting the right resources, and restraint from starting to implement too soon. If you've never opened a cafe before, find someone who has and ask their advice *before* you've spent half your savings. As Torbert writes:

> "So important is the existence of a peer network willing to invest time, energy, and intelligence, that a new organisation is much more likely to succeed if the originators have a prior career and an established peer network before they try to create their own organisation." (*Managing the Corporate Dream* p23-24)

Step Three (***Incorporation***) is about "producing products or services," establishing viability and proving itself within the resources available. Focus on doing what was promised with the people and cash available, with restraint from trying to do too much and running out of funds. Torbert writes, "At the incorporation stage, the foremost challenge is to set limits, meet deadlines, and cut out activities that are inconsistent with the original dream – in short, to create a mould." (*Managing the Corporate Dream* p65)

What *achieving viability* means in practice will depend on the organisation. For a business, fully completing *Incorporation* requires making a profit, but there may be interim milestones. For example, an internet start-up with costs of $500k a month and funding of $5m has ten months to either launch a new product and make some sales or demonstrate enough progress to raise further funding from investors. (Chapter 9 of *Action Inquiry* has a good case study on this issue.)

The other challenge at *Step Three* (*Incorporation*) is to stay true to the original conception or dream. In *Managing the Corporate Dream*, Torbert describes an architect's firm that was founded to "build flexible, easily adaptable, creativity-enhancing spaces for fast-growing companies." In its early days, to generate some cash, the firm took some commissions for residential housing, carried these out successfully, established a reputation and was rapidly "submerged with requests to do residential housing" (p48). Thus the firm had established financial viability, but had not been true to the spirit of the original idea.

In turns out there is a balance here: "one's original fantasies are more likely than not to contain elements of self-indulgence. The market disciplines that strip us of these self-indulgencies can be appreciated as spiritually liberating, enlightening, and sharpening. But the trick is to navigate the pressure of *Incorporation* in such a way as to slough off self-indulgence and, simultaneously, to realise the true kernel of the original dream." (*Managing the Corporate Dream*, p48)

Table 7.2 Discussion points for each step

Step One (Conception)	• How compelling is the dream? Does it meet an unmet need? Does it excite the founders or champions?
Step Two (Investments)	• How strong is the emotional commitment of the founders? • How good is their network? To what extent are they tapping their network?
Step Three (Incorporation)	• What's the right the right balance between staying true to the original dream versus adapting it to the realities of the situation? • Is the organisation sufficiently well focused, so it either reaches breakeven or shows enough progress with the resources it already has?
Step Four (Experiments)	• Is the organisation "truly experimenting – taking disciplined stabs in the dark – rather than merely trying one or two preconceived alternatives?" (*Action Inquiry* p128)
Step Five (Systematic Productivity)	During this period of legitimate focus on process- approach, measurement, and systematisation: • What is the human element, of both operations and the vision / mission? • To what extent is the organisation paying sufficient attention to this human element?
Step Six (Social Network)	• Is the shared vision and mission strong enough (i.e., sufficiently well shared and supported) to hold the organisation together in the face of the inevitable splintering forces introduced by the differing mindsets and the high levels of autonomy? How strong is the sense of "we are all better together here"? • Is the organisation at risk of flipping back to *Experiments*? Are there any respects in which it has already flipped back to *Experiments*?

At ***Step Four*** (***Experiments***), the organisation encourages the discussion and implementation of new ideas. Torbert writes:

"At the Experiments stage, the foremost challenge is to try new ways of doing business, new ways to make the dream come true as the organisation grows larger and the environment changes – in short, to break the mould." (*Managing the Corporate Dream* p65)

"Alternative administrative, production, selection, reward, financial, marketing, and political strategies practiced, tested in operation, and re-formed in rapid succession. Critical issues: truly experimenting – taking disciplined stabs in the dark – rather than merely trying one or two pre-conceived alternatives; finding a viable, longer-lasting combination of strategy and structure for the following stage." (*Action Inquiry* p128)

Step Five (*Systematic Productivity*) is, according to Torbert, "the whole point of organising, most people would say. At this stage, the organisation is finally doing at full throttle what it set out to do. Attention is tightly focused on consistent implementation of systematic procedures for accomplishing the predefined task. Objective, quantitative measurements for the marketability or political viability of the product or service become the overriding criteria of success." (*Managing the Corporate Dream* p91)

Nearly all businesses stop at *Systematic Productivity*, and thereafter seek further growth in revenue and profit margins, e.g. through expansion into new products, distribution channels and geographies.

Few organisations attempt to develop further to **Step Six (*Social Network*)**, and Chapter 3 explores possible motives for doing so. It involves the move from hierarchy to mutuality, which enables radical, counter-cultural experiments and different mindsets to flourish.

Each developmental step has its own challenges. Table 7.2 suggests critical questions for organisations at each step to discuss.

Applying the Step framework to Tesla Inc.

The *Conception* of Tesla Inc. began in 2000 after Martin Eberhard and Marc Tarpenning sold their ebook company, and sought to start another venture. In Business Insider[2], Drake Baer describes how they researched the electric car sector, which at the time was mainly for hobbyists. They encountered the "tzero", a fast sports car with powerful acceleration, and this inspired their vision.

Baer goes on to describe how in 2003 they practiced their sales pitch with venture capital investors unlikely to invest in it. These practice runs identified several issues they hadn't thought about: how the franchise dealership model works; navigating contentious political issues on the left and right; and how it would be much easier to use someone else's car model as a starting point. Testing and refining the idea like this is a vital part of *Conception*.

Late 2003 marks their transition from *Conception* to *Investments*. They began discussions with Lotus about using the Lotus Elise as the foundation for their car, and licenced technology from AC Propulsion. In 2004, with those problems resolved, they started their full pitches to venture capitalist firms.

They met Elon Musk in April 2004 who, Baer writes, shared their vision to "Make a vastly superior car, not just a car that sucks less". Musk invested $7.5m and became chairman.

Musk's investment marked the beginning of *Incorporation*, as Tesla now had the funds to hire designers and engineers, and start serious work with Lotus. By November 2004, they had a driveable "test mule" – a modified Lotus full of protype technology for evaluation.

During this *Incorporation* stage, Tesla's leadership had to balance three factors: staying true to their original dream of a vastly superior car; the realities of production and manufacturing; and showing enough progress to keep investors happy. Musk's influence was critical in keeping to the original dream of a premium car and raising capital from investors to keep the company going. Baer describes many decisions that ensured the car was desirable, but which added two years to its development. These included including lowering the Elise's doorsills, retooling its seats, changing the headlights and more. These delayed full production from 2006 to 2008.

Tesla produced the Roadster from Feb 2008 to December 2012 and sold 2,450 of them. In many ways it was a proof-of-concept car: manufactured by Lotus and based on the Elise, experiencing technical issues, and, as an electric two-seater sports car, a niche product. As a proof of concept for investors, though, it worked. Over these five years, Tesla raised $237m through its IPO and $283m in other rounds of financing.

The Model S, unveiled in 2008 and launched in 2012, was a major step forward. It was manufactured by Tesla itself, and as a five-door hatchback, had the potential to be a mass-market car. Creating a mass-market car had always been part of the Tesla dream.

From 2000 to 2012, Tesla's story fits well the stages of developmental theory. The founders had a compelling vision; they tested and refined it before seeking investors; they grappled with the trade-offs between staying true to their vision, managing the reality of operations, and showing enough progress to satisfy investors. Looking back, they balanced these factors successfully.

Had Tesla's story continued to follow developmental theory, its leadership would then have given priority to breaking even. The economics of the automotive industry are such that manufacturing costs per car come down sharply with scale. Tesla has typically sold about 4,500 Model S cars per month. If they could scale this to, say, 20,000 – 40,000 units per month, costs per unit could easily fall 30-40% and maybe much more. Ideally, Tesla would be in a virtuous circle, where sales went up, causing manufacturing costs per unit to fall, in turn allowing them to cut prices, in turn further boosting sales.

Table 7.3 Developmental milestones for Tesla

Step One (Conception)	• 2000: Eberhard and Tarpenning start seeking their next venture.
	• 2000: Eberhard discovers AC Propulsion's tzero.
	• 2003: vision in place for a two-seater electric sports car
	• 2003: start practice pitches to low potential investors. Uncover important issues they hadn't thought about.
Step Two (Investments)	• 2003: discussions with Lotus as a partner and AC Propulsion to licence technology.
	• 2004: begin proper pitches to potential investors.
	• 2004: meet Musk, who invests an initial $7.5m and becomes chairman of the board.
	• 2005: $13m series B funding.
	• 2006: $40m series C funding.
	• 2008: $40m debt financing.
	• 2010: IPO raising $227m.
	• 2012-17: 12 rounds of financing totalling over $11bn.
Step Three (Incorporation)	• 2004: serious work with Lotus begins. Hires engineers and designers.
	• 2004: test mule – drivable car with prototype technology and components.
	• 2006: Roadster prototype unveiled (two-seater sports car).
	• 2008: Roadster launch.
	• 2008: Model S unveiled (five-door hatchback)
	• 2009: first profitable month (July).
	• 2012: Model S launched; Roadster discontinued.
	• 2013: first profitable quarter.
Step Four (Experiments)	• 2010? work starts on Model X (sports utility vehicle).
	• 2012: Model X prototype unveiled.
	• 2015: Model X launched.
	• 2016: Model 3 prototype unveiled (four-door sedan).
	• 2016: acquisition of Solar City, a solar panel installer.
	• 2017: Model 3 launched.
	• 2017: Tesla Semi prototype unveiled (commercial truck).
	• 2019: Model Y prototype unveiled (compact utility vehicle).
	• 2019: Second generation Roadster unveiled.

Following such a strategy, Tesla would have focused on scaling production, ironing out manufacturing problems, keeping delivery waiting times low, and cutting prices as costs per unit came down. If successful, this would have allowed them to fully complete *Incorporation* by breaking even, and fully exit *Investments* by no longer needing to rely on capital investment to stay afloat.

Instead, Tesla's actions look more consistent with starting to advance *Experiments* while still anchored in *Investments* and *Incorporation* – see Table 7.3. Starting work on a sports utility vehicle was probably the beginning of Tesla's *Experiments* stage. The prototype Model X was unveiled in February 2012, which means work may have started in 2010. The Model X was launched in 2015. By 2016, when Tesla unveiled a four-door sedan, the Model 3, and acquired a solar panel installer for $2.6bn, the *Experiments* stage was at full speed.

To summarise, from around 2010 to at least 2019, Tesla was spread across three developmental stages:

- *Investments* because it was still relying on investor capital and had to go regularly to financial markets for more funds.
- *Incorporation* because it was still not able to scale production and make a regular profit.
- *Experiments* because it entered the SUV segment, acquired a solar panel installation company, and announced entry into CUV, commercial truck and sports car segments.

A strategy consistent with developmental theory would have focused on scaling production and achieving manufacturing efficiencies, not entering new segments. The risks with Tesla's actual strategy are that the new models distract its manufacturing division, making it harder for them to scale, that investors eventually lose patience, and that traditional car manufacturers come successfully into the market already having the ability to scale.

---

[2] *The Making of Tesla: Invention, Betrayal, and the Birth of the Roadster*, Drake Baer, Business Insider, November 2014.

Further aspects

PART THREE

FURTHER THEORETICAL ASPECTS

Further aspects

EIGHT

Conversational and organisational action-logics

More on Steps vs Levels

The two different aspects of the model – *Steps* where an organisation is intentionally passing through a stage, and *Levels* where an organisation has settled stably at a stage – can be one of the harder parts of the model to follow. Torbert's writings do not explicitly differentiate between the two, that's been introduced here.

Table 8.1 illustrates the difference, and also shows the model in different context, marriage. A *Step* organisation grapples with the challenges of a particular stage in a timely way, whereas the *Level* organisation, having settled stably, may be suffering from its downsides.

Figure 8.1

Level One	Level Two	Level Three	Level Four	Level Five	Level Six	Level Seven
Concept-ion	Invest-ments	Incorpor-ation	Experi-ments	Syst. Prod.	Social Network	Collab. Inquiry
Step One	Step Two	Step Three	Step Four	Step Five	Step Six	

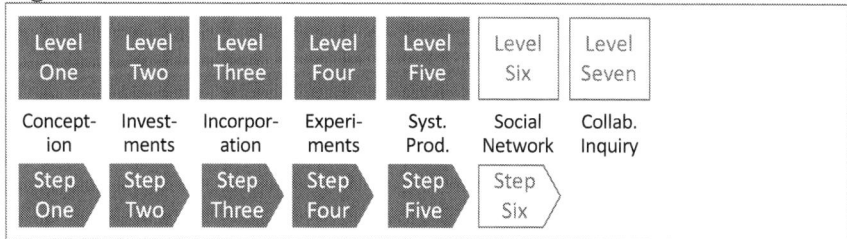

Just as there are *Step*-equivalents of the *Levels* introduced in part 1, there are also *Level*-equivalents of the *Steps* covered in part 2. A *Level One* organisation has settled stably at the idea stage – it never got off the ground. A *Level Two* organisation continually asks for support and investments, and may receive some, but never moves on to creating anything. One possibility is a company that carries on asking for funding, but is always turned down – the organisers should perhaps return to *Step One*, and re-evaluate its basic idea. A criminal gang might be classed as a kind of *Level Two* organisation: always taking from its environment, but never attempting to create any value itself.

Table 8.1: *Steps* and *Levels* in the context of a marriage

	Description of *Step* activities	Settling at the *Level*
One (Conception)	The agreement to get married, plus any discussions before or after about what their marriage would mean to them and how it might work in practice.	Exploring the idea of marriage but never reaching the point of getting engaged – though staying together in a relationship.
Two (Investments)	Preparing to get married, including preparing for the wedding, seeking support from relatives, and perhaps other aspects such as planning new living arrangements.	Stuck at engagement. Many PG Wodehouse novels have a plot that follows this narrative, e.g., a parent or guardian won't approve, the couple need to establish themselves financially, or one party is not fully committed.
Three (Incorporation)	The marriage ceremony itself, the wedding day, and perhaps the first few months (or years) of the marriage.	Unable to move to the next level, how the marriage works is undiscussable; even minor changes are never discussed; conflict is ignored and endured rather than addressed and resolved.
Four (Experiments)	The couple experiment with different ways of making the marriage work for them (but without challenging fundamental assumptions or their core identity).	Unable to move to the next level, the cumulative effect of all these experiments is the risk the couple's lives fragment. In time, perhaps they start to lead separate lives.
Five (Systematic Productivity)	The couple have established a way of living together that works for them. Both feel comfortable raising issues and suggesting changes (again without challenging fundamental assumptions or their core identity).	For some, there may be no disadvantages. Others may find the (unexamined and undiscussed) fundamental identity – perhaps one partner does nearly all the caregiving – constraining and unfulfilling.

Returning to the cafe examples, there is *The Level Three,* introduced in Chapter 1, and *The Step Three,* introduced here. Both *The Level Three* and *The Step Three* are at the *Incorporation* organisational action-logic. *The Level Three* has settled stably at this stage. *The Step Three* is grappling with the challenges of the action-logic in a timely way, while passing through to a later stage. In both cafes, discussion of the design or nature of the task is unwelcome, but their motivations and responses differ.

In response to the suggestion "how about we sell that new brand of coffee they're advertising at the moment," *The Level Three's* owners might respond, as described earlier, with "that's not how we do things around here" perhaps because new ideas are taken as criticism and make everybody uncomfortable. The owners of *The Step Three,* on the other hand, might say "look, we have three people, ten thousand dollars, and four weeks before we open. How about we just focus for the moment on getting ready for the 10th of next month and getting enough customers through the door so we can pay our suppliers and our people?" The difference is what makes the subject undiscussable. At *The Level Three*, it is an unconscious emotional response: new ideas make people uncomfortable. At *The Step Three*, it is a conscious rational choice: new ideas are a distraction at the time because the team needs to focus all its attention on the getting the cafe ready for opening.

In addition to *The Level Five*, there is *The Step Five*, and the differences are similar to *Level* and *Step Three*. Whereas *The Level Five* has settled stably at this action-logic, *The Step Five* is passing through *Systematic Productivity* and grappling with its challenges in a timely way.

At *The Level Five*, the leadership team would likely struggle to have meaningful discussions about double-loop changes that involve a change in mindset, for example:

- Jack's Welch's boundaryless idea, which he describes as removing the barriers between different functions, between national divisions, between businesses, their suppliers and their customers, making everyone "part of a single process." (*Jack*, p186)

- Self-managing teams, which Frederic Laloux describes in *Reinventing Organisations*. Aspects include "with no middle management and little staff, … organisations dispense with the usual control mechanisms; they are built on foundations of mutual trust… The heart of the matter is that workers and employees are seen as reasonable people that can be trusted to do the right thing. With that premise, very few rules and control mechanisms are needed." (p80)

- Full information transparency, also covered in *Reinventing Organisations*: "there are no unimportant people. Everybody expects to have access to all the information at the same time. It's a 'no secret' approach that extends to all data, including the most sensitive. This information includes not only financial data, but also salaries or the performance of individual teams." (p110)

The above ideas are outside the conventional mindset of typical organisations today. At *The Level Five,* the leadership team lacks the capacity or capability to explore such suggestions. As a result, they would likely ignore or dismiss them without discussion, and perhaps lowering their opinion of the people who raised the ideas.

At *The Step Five,* on the other hand, leaders are consciously choosing not to allow such discussions because the task at hand is establishing and solidifying a smooth-running operation. Their thought process may go something like this: "we still haven't nailed recruitment, and we'll need to find a replacement for our CFO who retires in six months. The teams in our five newest cafes are still gelling, so customer satisfaction can be a little shaky. I think we have enough on our hands right now without exploring major changes like these just yet."

Introducing conversational action-logics

Torbert's work on leadership distinguishes "*first-person* action-inquiry within ourselves," "*second-person* action-inquiry in our conversations with others," and "[*third-person*] action inquiry as a way of organising people, knowledge, and resources". Each of these has a corresponding action-logic, summarised in Table 8.2.

Table 8.2: First, second and third-person action-logics

Individual action-logics	Conversational action-logics	Organisational action-logics
Individual meaning-making and acting (First person)	The nature of the conversations that do and don't take place (Second person)	An organisation's structure, processes, and dynamics. (Third person)

The model of individual, first person, action-logics is pretty well known across different fields, including leadership education, action research, and developmental psychology. A *Harvard Business Review* article[3] about Torbert's model is now one of HBR's 10 must-reads on leadership. The model has also been written about by others (e.g. Kegan, Josephs & Joiner), deployed by several consulting firms, and is widely used in leadership development and coaching.

Table 8.3: Summary of individual, conversational and organisational action-logics

Individual action-logics (first person)		Conv. action-logics (second person)	Organisational action-logics (third person)	
Stage name(s)	Individual meaning-making and leadership competences (first person)	Nature of the conversations that do and don't take place (second person)	An organisation's structure, processes and dynamics (third person)	Stage name
Impulsive	Impulses rule behaviour.	Short and simple verbal exchanges, e.g. "hunt" or "water".	Chaotic.	Conception
Opportunist	*Wins any way possible.* Self-oriented; manipulative; "might makes right."	Conversations largely banter, jokes, threats, trivia, and orders.	Unstable hierarchical structure based on following orders from people with power.	Investments
Diplomat	*Avoids overt conflict.* Wants to belong; obeys group norms; rarely rocks the boat.	Not able or willing to discuss new ideas, changes to the work or how it is done.	Stable hierarchical structure based on following instructions from senior leaders.	Incorporation
Expert	*Rules by logic and expertise.* Seeks rational efficiency.	Able to discuss new ideas, and starting new activities. Starting activities is easier to discuss openly than stopping them.	Silos, fragmentation, complexity being spread too thinly.	Experiments
Achiever	*Meets strategic goals.* Effectively achieves goals through teams; juggles managerial duties and market demands.	Able to discuss the efficiency and effectiveness of the whole based on an understanding of cause and effect. At ease discussing starting *and* stopping activities.	Standardisation, shared services (e.g. common HR or IT functions serving multiple business units), prevalence of measures and targets.	System. Product.
Redefining	*Interweaves competing personal and company action logics.* Creates unique structures to resolve gaps b/w strategy and performance.	Able to question assumptions underlying assumptions and mindsets, and explore alternatives.	Autonomous, non-hierarchical units connected by shared vision and collaboration.	Social Network
Transforming	*Generates organizational and personal transformations.* Exercises the power of mutual inquiry, vigilance, and vulnerability for both the short and long term.	Shared reflection on vision... open rather than masked interpersonal relations... multiple kinds of feedback... paradoxes to be explored... discussion of structures appropriate to the moment.	The Teal practices described in *Reinventing Organisations*, such as self-management, information transparency, and elimination of staff functions.	Collab. Inquiry

The model of organisational, third person, action-logics has so far not reached the same popularity or prominence (though one careful review is that of Mark Edwards in his 2010 *Organizational Transformation for Sustainability*). This work further develops the organisational model, with Torbert's support and under his review, changing the way it's presented and introducing, among other things, the distinction between *Step* and *Level*.

This work also introduces *conversational action-logics* and proposes these as the main mediating mechanism between individuals and organisations, that is to say that conversations are the bridge between individual leadership competences and organisational structure, dynamics and performance. This angle has several implications.

First, it offers a new angle for leadership development and coaching – specifically, new topics to discuss with colleagues and new agenda points to propose for group meetings. This is a possible resolution to the challenge of measuring return on investment in leadership development and coaching. "Jenny did that coaching and as a result prompted us to start talking about X. If she hadn't done that, we'd never have prioritised initiative Y, and that's been of huge value to us."

Second, it offers a new lever for organisational transformation that directly integrates culture and structure. According to Edwards, many writers emphasise either culture or structure at the expense of the other, and this doesn't work. He writes:

"[of] the debate between theorists who see organisational culture (collective interiors) as the central explanatory concept for transformation and those who see organisational systems and structures (collective exteriors) as the main player in change... Culture and structure, the informal interior and the formal exterior aspects of organising, complement and support each other and together form two ends of an important conceptual lens for exploring transformation.

"Several researchers of organisational change have commented on the very poor results of programmes that focus purely on transforming organisational culture or, alternatively, on the restructuring of organisational operations and systems (Applebaum & Wohl, 2000; Forster, 2005, Kotter, 1995). ... Focusing on the exterior, objective aspects of organisations can result in the dominance of outcomes over process, in measurement over meaning, products over people and in sales over service. On the other hand, a heavy focus on organisational culture can result in a lack of structure, accountability and decisiveness." (*Organisational Transformation for Sustainability*, pp137-138)

The lever proposed here – conversations – affects both culture and structure. Introducing new kinds of conversations will, over time and with persistence, directly influence an organisation's culture. And the conversations themselves will, over time and with persistence, cause changes in the organisation's structures and systems. Introducing a new kind of conversation is a double-loop learning change for organisations, so it will likely be resisted. Just a few conversations is unlikely to be enough.

A third implication is that by overlooking the role of conversations as a bridge between individual leadership and organisational change, the transformation power of new initiatives is lost. For example, someone at the *Achiever* individual action-logic will likely pay attention to how well their organisation works as a whole. They may start conversations on the subject, and one possible outcome of the conversations is a decision to create balanced scorecard. The balanced scorecard (third person structure or process) is a result of the conversation (second person), which in turn follows from individual meaning-making and leadership (first person). In the other direction, the balanced scorecard should then stimulate further conversations about how well the organisation works a whole, which in turn might help individuals in the organisation develop to the *achiever* action-logic.

Except this is not usually how it works. What is more likely to happen (in this author's experience) is that someone senior, probably at the *Achiever* action-logic, proposes a balanced scorecard and convinces their colleagues, but without the explicit goal of helping the organisation work well as a whole. The design of the balanced scorecard doesn't give this sufficient emphasis, and the conversations don't happen when the scorecard is launched. People in the organisation then treat the scorecard as just another KPI report, but with a fancy name and a particular structure. The full transformation power of the balanced scorecard – to stimulate new kinds of conversation, to help people develop to the *achiever* action-logic, to help the organisation actually work better as a whole – is largely lost.

Necessary conditions

Developmental theory predicts:
- To reach a particular conversational action-logic, a team needs at least one member at the corresponding individual action-logic.
- To reach a particular organisational action-logic, an organisation needs at least one team at the corresponding conversational action-logic.

These conditions are necessary, but not sufficient. Regarding the first, if the team is hierarchical, the action-logic of the most senior member is likely to dominate. The conversation may occasionally reach a later level, but the interventions of the senior member will regularly bring the conversation back to their own level. The greater the authority of the senior member and the more hierarchical the team, the stronger this effect will be.

Regarding the second condition, the conversational action-logics of the highest-ranking teams are likely to dominate. For many organisations, these will be the executive leadership team and board of directors.

Putting these two factors together, the action-logic of the CEO, i.e. the highest-ranking person in the highest-ranking team, will be of critical importance. If the CEO's action-logic is *Expert*, the team or organisation will be unlikely to develop fully to *Systematic Productivity*. For example, in one organisation, an observer estimated the CEO's action-logic as *Expert*. The organisation was the result of the merger of two businesses. The whole rationale for the organisation's existence was based on the two divisions working well together, and the whole strategy depended their ability to create joint products and services and sell to each other's customers.

The way the CEO managed the divisional presidents prevented this from happening. In brief, if one division sold the other's products and services, the revenue could be counted twice – towards both divisions' revenue target, with the double counting eliminated in group consolidation. But the profit could only be counted once, which meant at least one division would have to accept lower profit margins, and this was unacceptable in the management climate at the time. The CEO, with an Expert action-logic, was unable to resolve this tension. The entire strategy, which depended on *Systematic Productivity* dynamics, failed. The CEO eventually left the business and the organisation was split back in two.

The action-logics, both individual and conversational, of the board of directors also matters. Dennis Bakke was CEO of AES, one of the teal (*Collaborative Inquiry*) organisations profiled in *Reinventing Organisations*. In *Joy at Work*, Bakke describes how, when the share price was high, the board of directors were vocal supporters of the company's values and decentralised decision making. But when the share price was low, the board lost confidence in the values-driven approach. As one of Bakke's colleagues told him, "they [the values] didn't work, Dennis. We need to adjust." Bakke perceived that others had supported the values only because they were good for morale and generated publicity, rather than "because they were intrinsically right" (*Joy of Work* pp69-70).

Lest it all seem too formulaic, Mark Edwards advises caution in analysing organisational change solely through the lens of developmental stages. There are many other lenses – his book describes 24 – and any one lens brings some dynamics sharply into focus and may obscure others. Developmental stage models, in his view, tend to overlook the potential for social mediation, which "occurs in the exchanges between two or more social entities, for example, in the relationships between individuals or between organisations in industry groups" (*Organisational Transformation for Sustainability* p119).

Edwards offers two examples to illustrate the complex dynamics possible in the relationship between individuals and organisations. Gandhi's salt march "was an act of nonviolent civil disobedience… had a significant effect on changing world and British attitudes towards Indian sovereignty and self-rule and caused large numbers of Indians to join the fight for the first time…. over 60,000 Indians were jailed" (Wikipedia). Edwards suggests that Gandhi's words and action communicated directly to the best in each person. They were inspired by him to risk imprisonment, injury and death for their cause. This created a group dynamic of enormous, yet non-violent, power from participants who were typically unprivileged, low income, and with little education.

Edwards contrasts this with the Stanford prison experiment where students participated as either guards or prisoners in a prison simulation. "Some participants developed their roles as the officers and enforced authoritarian measures and ultimately subjected some prisoners to psychological torture. Many of the prisoners passively accepted psychological abuse and, by the officers' request, actively harassed other prisoners who tried to stop it." (Wikipedia). Here – though the validity of the results have since been challenged – the social relations created a brutal group dynamic from participants who were some of the most privileged, best educated students in the US.

In business, action-logics are weak at explaining how double-loop change can sweep across an industry sector, profession or job function. Developments such just-in-time manufacturing, business process outsourcing, agile software development, solution selling and experiential learning, among many others, involve major changes in mindset. These developments did not become prevalent because most organisations are capable of double-loop learning, but rather through social mediation. People hear about the next big thing of the moment: it's what consultants promote, conference organisers put on their agendas, journalists and bloggers write about, leading companies try out, and ambitious managers want to work on.

---

3 *Seven Transformations of Leadership*, David Rooke and William R. Torbert, Harvard Business Review, April 2005.

NINE

Other aspects of the theory

Organisations reinventing themselves

Torbert predicted the existence of teal organisations in 1987, and described them as follows:

"At the *Collaborative Inquiry* stage, organisations not only produce goods or services but do so in ways whereby members continually reexplore the authority and legitimacy of the organisation's various structures, strategies and systems, with a regular process for amending them. The organisation *is* no longer any particular structure. It *has* structures. And it has inquiry systems for restructuring, and it is these with which identifies more closely.

"The organisation at this stage of development deliberately fosters inquiry about its mission and about whether its structure, operations, and social outcomes are consistent with its mission and are beneficial. In other words, the question of whether the organisation functions so as to make the corporate dream come true begins, for the first time, to become explicitly and to be tested as part of the regular functioning of the organisation." (*Managing the Corporate Dream* p119)

"… its identity becomes lodged less in its current structure than in its capacity for restructuring. It becomes capable of restructuring to meet unforeseeable market and political conditions, restructuring as subgroups within the organisation develop, and restructuring to more consistently enact the corporate dream." (*ibid* p121)

He described their specific characteristics as:

- "Explicit shared reflection about the corporate dream/mission and actuality/history in the wider social context (recapitulating *Conception*)
- Open rather than masked interpersonal relations, with disclosure,

support and confrontation of apparent value differences (recapitulating *Investments*)

- Systematic evaluation and feedback of corporate and individual performance on multiple indexes (recapitulating *Incorporation*)
- Direct facing and creative resolution of paradoxes (which otherwise become polarised conflicts); inquiry-productivity, freedom-control, quantity-quality, and so forth (recapitulating *Experiments* [and *Social Network*])
- Interactive development of, and commitment to, unique self-amending strategies and structures appropriate to this particular organisation at this particular historical moment (recapitulating *Systematic Productivity*)" (*ibid* p128)

With these features of regularly revisiting steps one to six, a *Collaborative Inquiry* organisation is able to regularly reinvent itself. As Torbert puts it:

"It is not by chance that the five characteristics of *Collaborative Inquiry* describe a process of transformation rather than a 'steady state' logic arrived at after some transformation. In moving toward *Collaborative Inquiry* and still later stages, an organisation is developing dynamic structures, strategies, and systems that recognise and support appropriate transformations rather than resisting them." (*ibid* p129)

Torbert's work and Laloux's *Reinventing Organisations* are highly complementary. Torbert's work provide a theoretical framework, and a conceptual analysis of dynamics, causes and effects. Laloux's empirical research reveals how these theoretical features manifest themselves in "concrete, day-to-day practices". Both Torbert and Laloux agree on necessary conditions: the people with authority need to have reached the required stage of individual development.

Laloux's work looks more at the end result: what does the organisation look like once it has transformed. Torbert's work – see Chapters 10 and 11 of *Action Inquiry* – provides more insights into the nature of the journey to get there. Torbert brings out rather than hides the inevitable messiness and bumpiness in the journey. Laloux makes it seem much easier: "if a CEO truly wants the shift to happen, and offers the right presence, it *will* happen" (*Reinventing Organisations* p284). This author wondered if readers of *Reinventing Organisations* might end up underestimating the nature of the challenge.

Relationship between conversational and organisational action-logics

The second-person, conversational and third-person, organisational action-logics of any group will not always be aligned. If the conversational action-logic is at a later stage, this might be a *Step* organisation (see table 9.1). The other possibility, for example if a new leadership team has been appointed, is that the third person structures and processes of the organisation will start changing as a result of the new types of conversation.

Table 9.1: alignment between conversational and organisational action-logics

Conversational A-L later stage than Organisational A-L	•	Might be a *Step* organisation. It could start having particular kinds of conversations but is choosing not to have them. It could transform relatively easily to the next *Step* by relaxing that restraint.
Conversational and Organisational A-Ls at same stage	•	This is a *Level* organisation. It's organisation action-logics has reached the latest possible stage given its conversational capabilities. Transforming to the next *Level* is likely to require a major change initiative.
Conversational A-L earlier stage than Organisational A-L	•	Risk of dysfunction.

When the conversational and organisational action-logics are aligned, it is a typical *Level* organisation.

It's when the conversational action-logic is at an earlier stage that problems occur. Chapter 2 describes the possible problems when a shared services function (*Level Five* structure and process) does not operate at that conversational action-logic. Laloux offers this example:

"Because [the practice of defining a set of shared values and a mission statement] is in good currency, leaders in [*Level Five (Systematic Productivity)*] organisations increasingly feel obliged to have a task force come up with some values and a mission statement. But looking to values and mission statements to inform decisions only makes sense [*at Level Six (Social Network)*]. In [*Systematic Productivity*] organisations the yardstick for decisions is success: *Let's go with what will deliver top- or bottom-line results…* leadership might pay lip service to the values, but when the rubber hits the road and leaders have to choose between profits and values, they will predictably go for the former. They cannot uphold a practice and a culture (in this case a values-driven culture) that stems from a later stage of development." (*Reinventing Organisations* p41)

The model at different scales

The model can be used across a wide range of scales. At the micro level, it might be applied to a project, event, marriage, family, or small business. A project, for example, might follow the *Steps* as follows:

- Step One (Conception): spend time discussing and refining the idea before you start asking people for help or funds.

- Step Two (Investments): spend time asking people for help or funds before wasting inadequate funds.
- Step Three (Incorporation): use what resources you have to prove you can deliver before embarking on grander schemes.

The mid-level, sometimes called "meso," includes large businesses and institutions, and this is the primary focus of this work.

At the larger macro-level, organisational action-logics could be used to analyse subjects such as the European Union, Christianity, the global economy, and so on. In the case of the global economy, an *Experiments* mindset might mean that each country feels the need to have its own steel industry, national car manufacturer, national airline and so on. A global move to *Systematic Productivity* – while noting the disadvantages described in Part A – could include trends such as outsourcing English-language call centres to Jamaica, India, and the Philippines, the growth of China as the world's factory, and growth in global brands with a corresponding loss of national variety.

If this analysis holds true, anti-globalisation campaigners have available three broad strategies: try to keep the world economy at *Experiments*, resisting these trends to *Systematic Productivity* (e.g. economic nationalism); accept the global shift to *Systematic Productivity*, but try to change how that shift takes place to limit its disadvantages; or try to accelerate a shift towards *Social Network*, in the hope that such later-level thinking might combine strengths from both earlier levels.

TEN

Levels eight and nine

Level Eight (Foundational Community of Inquiry)

Level Eight is a rare kind of conversation – this section focuses on the conversational rather than organisational aspects, as the former will be vastly more practical and relevant to organisations. It begins by trying to convey the nature of the conversation, and then considers possible applications for a well-known company, Facebook.

Figure 10.1

Level One	Level Two	Level Three	Level Four	Level Five	Level Six	Level Seven	Level Eight	Level Nine
Concept-ion	Invest-ments	Incorpor-ation	Experi-ments	Syst. Prod.	Social Network	Collab. Inquiry	Comm. of Inquiry	Lib. Discipl.
Step One	Step Two	Step Three	Step Four	Step Five	Step Six	Step Seven	Step Eight	Level Nine

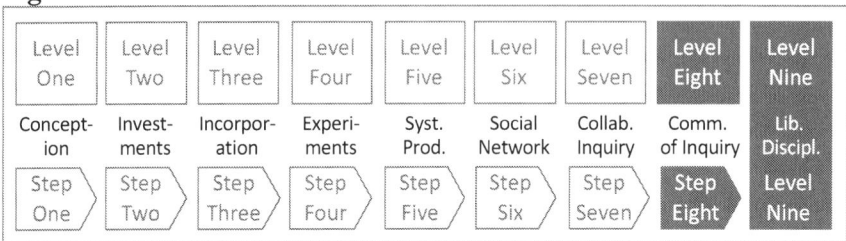

William Isaacs is one of the few people to have worked with and written about *Level Eight* conversations, which he calls *generative dialogue*. Isaacs has helped many clients work with generative dialogue and his book, *Dialogue and the Art of Thinking Together,* draws on examples from Ford Motor Company, Shell Oil, the healthcare sector, steel industry, and others. He describes this kind of conversation as follows:

"[Generative dialogue] is the rarest of all the spaces. It is the one where people cross over into awareness of the primacy of the whole... It is also a time when genuinely new possibilities come into being... this is a space where people generate new rules for interaction, where they are personally included but are also fully aware of the impersonal elements of their participation... Synchronicities arise more often here: one person will think of something and another will say it. People become more aware, in essence, of the primacy of the undivided whole that links us all, and so notice it more readily.

"In this fourth space, traditionally held positions are sufficiently loosened that very new possibilities can come into existence… The experience of an atmosphere large enough to accommodate radically different points of view without requiring any of them to change is a fundamental quality of this space. In it, many new possibilities and options can be seen that were hidden before." (pp279-280)

"… the silence is whole and, at times, sacred. The wisdom of the wider group takes precedence over the chatter of the individual." (p288)

Torbert describes the same dynamic as follows:

"[Members of a *Foundational Community of Inquiry* are] explicitly trying to co-create a setting – be it a business or family setting, a professional, a cultural, or a spiritual setting – where inquiry about the most difficult issues is valued and practiced and where suffering is shared and transformed." (*Action Inquiry* p193)

"At this developmental point [the organisation is not] based on, nor finds its identity in, a particular mindset or structure. Instead the organisation continually re-tastes the four 'territories of experience' [visioning strategising, performing and outcomes-assessing] – freshly seeking harmony among them.

"The transformation is… to having a reframing spirit. A reframing spirit continually overcomes itself, divesting itself of its own presuppositions. A reframing mind continually re-attunes itself to the frames of reference held by other actors in a situation, and to the underlying organisational and historical rhythms, seeking the 'common sense' of the situation, seeking to discover and articulate the motivating challenge of the situation in a language accessible to all participants.

"Discovering this motivating challenge can create a social jiu-jitsu effect: just as total disintegration is threatening, the person or organisation or nation suddenly fluidifies and acts with unforeseeable vigour and resolve. For this reason, this vulnerable power is often experienced as alchemist-like, witch-like, or clown-like." (*Personal and Organisational Transformations* p164)

M. Scott Peck calls these conversations *community*, and writes about them in *The Different Drum*. His experiences are in more personal or social contexts rather than organisational or business ones:

"… a soft quietness descends… The room is bathed in peace. Then, quietly, a member begins to talk about herself. She is being very vulnerable. She is speaking of the deepest part of herself. The group hangs on each word…

"When she is finished there is a hush. It goes on for a long time. But it does not seem long. There is no uneasiness in this silence. Slowly, out of the silence, another member begins to talk. He too is speaking very deeply, very personally, about himself. He is not trying to heal or convert the first person…" The description continues on p103 of *The Different Drum*.

This kind of human interaction may need to be experienced directly, as in "you had to be there." Isaacs writes, "One other important feature of this conversational space is the discovery many people make that they simply do not have the words to describe the experience that emerges." (p283)

To tackle the challenge of trying to convey what may need to be experienced directly, this section imagines possible *Level Eight* conversations at Facebook. Facebook's corporate mission statement for its first ten years was "to give people the power to share and make the world more open and connected." In 2017, the company changed this to "to give people the power to build community and bring the world closer together." Both versions are lofty in their ambition and have implications not just for Facebook's product or service, but also for the company's own actions and behaviours.

Consider issues where Facebook and parts of society disagree. One such issue is data privacy. Facebook's entire business model rests on offering advertisers the ability to narrowly target particular groups of consumers, and to do this it needs to gather and use data about what people are interested in. Privacy advocates on the other hand are deeply concerned about the direction and implications of this. Another issue is the kinds of content that Facebook allows people to share. On nudity in images, for example, there are at least three constituencies: those especially concerned with sexual equality, and who object to rules such allowing men's nipples to be shown, but not women's; those especially concerned with keeping Facebook safe for families and who are worried out it being overwhelmed by pornography; and Facebook itself, which needs a policy and process that can be understood by users and thousands of moderators worldwide.

Facebook has different options for engaging with consumer groups on topics like these. One approach would be to make all decisions behind closed doors, announce policies not always with 100% candour, defend its position absolutely in the media, show no signs of listening to other parties, and make any changes apparently grudgingly and only in response to huge pressure. The trouble with this approach is that Facebook would risk people becoming disenchanted with it, perceiving Facebook to be out of touch and not relevant to them. The Facebook brand and business would suffer, and its vision – "People use Facebook to stay connected with friends and family, to discover what's going on in the world, and to share and express what matters to them"

– would become that much harder to achieve.

A second problem is this approach is not true to Facebook's mission. Applying Facebook's mission to its own behaviours and actions, the first version begs the question, "if Facebook wishes an open and connected world, how open is Facebook itself, and how well connected is it to the various constituencies it wishes to serve?" The second version invites "to what extent do Facebook's own actions and behaviours bring Facebook itself closer to different parts of society?" Facebook's actions in the above approach distance itself from groups of society rather than bringing it closer together.

Suppose Facebook were willing to engage with different interest groups in a radically different way: to be willing to listen, to be open, to explore, to come "closer together"? Were it to do this, who knows what inventive and unexpected resolutions Facebook and different interest groups might stumble across. Who knows what impact this might have on Facebook's perceived relevance and connection to the world.

For difficult issues like data privacy and policies on contentious content, ordinary conversations are unlikely to rise to the challenge. Facebook would listen to and understand different parties, only to confirm what they already knew, that the parties have deeply held and incompatible views. This is the kind of situation that calls for a *Level Eight* conversation, generative dialogue.

To provide some clues to what that might involve in practice, here is Isaacs describing generative dialogue in action at a steel company:

"A few years ago a group of colleagues and I from MIT were invited to one of America's largest steel mills to introduce managers and steelworkers to a new way of talking together, to help them break through many years of intense division and strife." (*Dialogue and the Art of Thinking Together* page 6)

"Over a period of years our MIT research team worked with these steel workers and with the senior managers of the company – two groups with a history of deep, bitter labour disputes between them – to find a way of conversing that would transform some of their deepest differences into meaningful, useful dialogue. After some months, many of them experienced a radical change, one that – for a time at least – turned their swords into ploughshares. We delved into the deep assumptions carried by both groups and as a result forged great mutual respect, coordination and connection. Moreover this mutual understanding was extended to action in the form of improved performance, fewer grievances, and, for the first time in generations, mutual action to solve chronic problems in the mill. The changed atmosphere helped to convince outside financial groups to invest over $100m in the business. And despite the actions of people who sought to stop these explorations, many of the initiatives continue today." (*ibid* pages 8-9)

"At an annual meeting of MIT's Centre for Organisational Learning, five managers and five union steelworkers talked about what they had learned after six months of dialogue. A group of about 125 managers from leading companies around the United States listened to them. That the managers and union workers were able to sit together and talk openly and respectfully of one another about what they had achieved was enormously impressive. After all, here were two groups that had mistrusted each other for decades; now they were thinking together. They spoke freely and un-rehearsed. More than one person said later that tears came to his eyes.

"Toward the end of the presentation, one manager from a high-tech industry challenged their apparent success: 'you seem to have your team working well here. But what about shocks from the wider system? The price of steel, the price of scrap metal, the environment? How do you plan to overcome that hurdle?' No one replied for a long while. Then Conrad, the vice president of the local union said, 'well we don't really have a plan. We just take things one step at a time.'

"He went on. 'You know, sitting up here has been very uncomfortable for us. We do not usually do presentations like this. We were not sure what would happen. But I now see that we have a container [of openness and trust] that is large enough even to include all of you.' There was no bluster or defensiveness in his words, he simply drew a larger circle. Our authentic voice can set a new order of things, open new possibilities. It comes out even more clearly in dialogue, where the challenge is to speak the new word. And to do so that very moment. Conrad took the 'external shock' of the high-tech manager's comment to the group and included it in the same fashion they were including and dealing with all their problems." (pages 160-161)

Further aspects of *Level Eight (Foundational Community of Inquiry)*

Three books going into detail on *Level Eight* conversations are Isaacs's *Dialogue and the Art of Thinking Together,* Peck's *The Different Drum* and Torbert's *Creating a Community of Inquiry: Conflict, Collaboration, Transformation.* None is adequate as a how-to manual because no book could ever be adequate as a how-to manual. Isaacs writes, "Writing a book about [generative] dialogue is in some respects a contradiction in terms." Peck emphasises that you cannot create community, you can only create the conditions from which community can emerge. Torbert's developmental theory predicts that *Level Eight* conversations require leadership including someone profiling at the *Alchemical* individual action-logic.

Peck and Isaacs offer comparable four-step models for reaching *Level Eight,* summarised in Table 10.1. The first row, pseudocommunity or politeness, represents comfort zone or established norms. In the model of this paper, this comfort zone could be at any developmental stage or conversational action-logic, e.g. *Level Three (Incorporation)* or *Level Seven (Collaborative Inquiry)*. The second row, chaos or breakdown, is when the established norms break down and when people start saying what's really on their mind, often in frank or heated terms. This is a stage of discomfort. The challenge for the group is then to advance to emptiness or inquiry rather than fall back to the relative comfort of pseudocommunity or politeness.

Table 10.1: Peck's and Isaac's models for how group dynamics evolve to *Level Eight*

Peck's stages towards community	Isaacs' fields towards generative dialogue
Pseudocommunity – politeness and conflict avoidance.	**Politeness** – "People bring with them a set of inherited norms about how to interact… in this conversational field people do not surface what they 'really' think and feel." (p257, 259)
Chaos – open disagreement as members try to win the argument and convert others.	**Breakdown** – "people begin to say what they think… people begin to battle over whose meaning will have more power." (p265)
Emptiness – people drop their need to win arguments and convert others, and become more open to examining their own assumptions and views	**Inquiry** – "The energy changes… spirit of *curiosity*… people begin to notice and explore their assumptions… people do not feel compelled to have to agree… ideas tend to flow freely…" (p272, 273)
Community – "An extraordinary amount of healing and converting begins to occur – now that no one is trying to convert or heal." (p103-104)	**Generative Dialogue** – "an atmosphere large enough to accommodate radically different points of view without requiring any of them to change… many new possibilities and options can be seen that were hidden before." (p280)

(Note: despite surface similarities, these four phases are materially different to Bruce Tuckman's 1965 model of group development: forming, storming, norming, performing.)

Lastly, Table 10.2 shows some parallels between an individual's transformation to the *Alchemical* action-logic and a group's entry into *Level Eight (Foundational Community of Inquiry)*.

Table 10.2: Comparing individual and group transformation to *Alchemical* and *Level Eight*

Individual transformation to *Alchemical*	Group transformation to *Level Eight*
Allowing emptiness and meaninglessness into their lives	Go through an emptiness stage (Peck) or through a crisis of emptiness (Isaacs).
Sees directly for him/herself not just that their current personal identity or sense of self has become a limiting factor, but that any personal identity or sense of self must be a limiting factor.	A shared sense of spirit / underlying emotional need emerges, and the group sees that no fixed structure could satisfactorily realise this or meet its challenges. "Structure fails" (*Action Inquiry* p127)
Dissolving of psychological boundaries within the individual, integration with – owning – one's shadow energies*	Dissolving of psychological boundaries within the group, i.e., between people – "cross-over into the primacy of the whole… one person will think something, another will say it" (Isaacs pp279-280)
Weakening of psychological boundaries between the person and their environment.	Weakening of psychological boundaries between the group and its environment.
A willingness to trust the process, be true to oneself rather than attached to any particular outcome.	"One must quickly empty oneself of expectations if anything new is to happen… our expectations are not going to be met, and we cannot fully control the outcome we want to produce" (Isaacs p263)

* A possible visual representation is Bill Watterson's depiction of "evil Calvin"

Level Nine (Liberating Disciplines)

Little has been written about the last level in Torbert's model, and it will only be touched on here. Chapter 15 of *Personal and Organisational Transformations through Action Inquiry* by Fisher, Rooke and Torbert describes it (p183) as follows:

> "This final chapter offers a definition and illustration of the latest stage of organisation development, according to the theory espoused in this book. Few organisations in history can be said to have approached this stage, yet it is important to say something about this stage, for it represents the most complete realisation of a learning organisation that we can imagine. We call this stage *Liberating Disciplines*.
>
> "Liberating disciplines cultivate a spirit of inquiry and transformation

among organisational members who may first enter it at very different stages of personal development. Gradually the organisation's overall mission becomes a question that alerts and guides its members at each moment. Such an organisational structure does not just implement particular strategies and projects, but also questions whether given strategies, actions, and outcomes truly further the mission. The leadership of an organisation at this most advanced *Liberating Disciplines* stage of development can only sustain this subtle structure if the leaders themselves are at the parallel *Ironic* stage of development and have generated their own *Foundational Community of Inquiry*. Only then will the organisation cultivate, not members' obedient conformity, nor merely competent performance by members, but rather their continuing transformation from stage to stage of adult development as they increase their capacities to join in the inquiry."

Later in the chapter (p187), the authors take a formal definition of an organisation and invert it to describe *Liberating Disciplines*. The formal definition, simplified here, is from Katz and Kahn, and Table 10.3 shows its inversion:

"An organisational context is by definition a set of restrictions for focusing attention, narrowing cognitive style and limiting degrees of freedom."

Table 10.3: Describing *Liberating Disciplines* by inverting the definition of an organisation

An organisational context	A liberating discipline
is by definition	is by experience
a set of restrictions	a set of challenges
for focusing attention,	for questioning (the quality of one's) attention,
narrowing	and widening it and
cognitive style	one's cognitive-emotional tracking to include the enacted task, process and mission
and limiting degrees of freedom	and expanding degrees of freedom

Source: Simplified version of table on p187 of *Personal and Organisational Transformations*. The definition of organisation on the left side (simplified here) is from Katz and Kahn's authoritative 1978 book, *The Social Psychology of Organizations*.

To try to convey a sliver of *Liberating Disciplines*, imagine you are a leader in such an organisation. One of the tasks you have chosen to carry out yourself is to design activities that will, in the context of interpersonal relationships and group situations: stimulate self-awareness among participants; challenge participants' meaning-making (i.e., how they understand a situation and the significance they attach to different aspects); and encourage participants to try out new behaviours to make them more effective. Imagine further that the majority of participants are undergraduate business school students and you are Assistant Professor at the business school.

One of the activities you design for students is to write a series of learning papers. You instruct the students to pick an experience and write about four aspects: their behaviour in the situation; their feelings throughout the experience; an analysis of the situation using a theory that provides some insight into it; and, based on these reflections, a proposal for a new behaviour to try out.

You (at your later action-logic) designed this task with a particular intent: stimulate self-awareness, challenge meaning-making, and encourage new behaviours. The students, however, (at earlier action-logics) will likely interpret the significance of the task differently, and approach it with different (unconscious) intents. Consider, for a moment, how you yourself might have approached such a task in your early-to-mid twenties:

You might, in your early-to-mid twenties, if you were typical (and certainly like this author), have approached the task with the (completely unconscious) intent of avoiding pain or uncomfortable emotions, and preserving at all costs the self-image you had at the time. You might then have adopted the strategy of presenting yourself in a good light, demonstrating you were a mature and capable adult (within your existing and unexamined frame of maturity and capability). And in terms of your actions, perhaps you picked a situation that was well within your comfort zone, or maybe you framed the situation to make it clear others were to blame, or chose some other tactic that demonstrated your competence. As a result of all this, any conclusions you reached regarding new behaviours to try out were not the result of any meaningful reflection.

Returning to the story of you in the present day as a leader within this *Liberating Disciplines* organisation, one of the characteristics of leadership at this level is that you foresaw all of the above. You realised that "most subordinates would initially interpret the organisational structure and particular events based on a different model of reality (a different stage of development) from the one inspiring the leadership" (*Power of Balance* p102). Torbert gives this as an example of practicing deliberate irony.

Since you expected all this, you created a scoring method and feedback loop that confounded the students' intent and meaning-making, and thwarted their strategy. Your scoring method initially gave students points for describing any kind of emotion (and not if they didn't), and points for proposing a new behaviour to try that linked to the experience (and not if they didn't).

(Later rounds added two more scoring criteria.)

Had this author been enrolled on your course, he would have picked an experience within his comfort zone, described opinions rather than feelings, presented himself in a good light, and chosen superficial rather than challenging new behaviours to try – and have considered his response an excellent, "mature and adult" response. You, as the organiser, would have marked his paper a fail; you would have provided detailed written feedback, and asked him to rewrite and resubmit.

This illustrates a second characteristic of *Liberating Disciplines*: the creation of tasks that, when participants tackle them within the pure meaning-making of their (earlier) action-logic, will necessarily fail. For example, after several attempts at presenting themselves in a good light, after several resulting "fail" grades and requests to resubmit, and after receiving several iterations of detailed written feedback, the student at last accepts that the "good light" strategy does not work, and instead he or she must tackle writing about their anxieties, fears, uncertainties, and lack of perfection. Thus the nature of the task forces – truly compels – alignment with the task designer's intent before the student can succeed. Torbert calls this "epistemological transparency" or "tasks that are incomprehensible and undoable without reference to the accompanying processes and purposes" (*Power of Balance* p102).

Some students then challenge you on the approach and premises of the learning paper itself. How might you respond? In this organisation, you decide to encourage their challenge, thereby making yourself vulnerable to a different approach. You invite them to write their papers based on any other learning theory of their choice, while explaining the advantages of that alternative theory. This illustrates another characteristic of *Liberating Disciplines*: "conditional openness to challenge."

The above story reflects Torbert's real-world experiences of teaching as he describes them in Chapter 5 of *Power of Balance*. In the actual scenario, 44% of students got no credit for their first learning paper (where they only had to fulfil two of the assignment criteria), and were asked to rewrite and resubmit. By the end of the course, by which time the marking required learning papers to fulfil all four criteria, 98% of students were passing.

All this is intended to convey just a facet of *Level Nine* (*Liberating Disciplines*). Indeed in *Personal and Organisational Transformations,* the authors quote a colleague of theirs, Peter Reason, as saying "We can only fully comprehend a liberating community or organisation as we experience it. However we can say that such communities encourage their members through a discipline of practice to question…"

(There's a *Liberating Discipline* exercise readers can try out by themselves. Eugene Gendlin describes the six-step method in his short book *Focusing,* and Torbert taught it at Yale. The method allows people to access "an internal knowing which is directly experienced but is not yet in words. Focusing can, among other things, be used to become clear on what one feels or wants, to obtain new insights about one's situation, and to stimulate change or healing of the situation." (Wikipedia))

ELEVEN

Supporting evidence, scope for further research, testable predictions, terminology

Supporting evidence, scope for further research, testable predictions

Perhaps there are three possible types of support for any model: theoretical support, empirical support, and support by analogy.

Torbert describes the theoretical support for organisational action-logics as follows:

> "These stages of organisational development were originally defined by Torbert (1974) by comparing nine different stage theories of interpersonal, group or organisational development (e.g., Bennis 1964; Dunphy 1968; Erikson 1959; Greiner 1972; Lippitt and Schmidt 1967; Mills 1964) to a close analysis of five organising cycles in one organisation. This new multistage theory of organisational development offered richer descriptions of both early and later stages than other organisation development theories at that time (Greiner 1972; Lippitt and Schmidt 1967) and than later organisational life cycle theories (Cameron and Whetten 1983; Quinn and Cameron 1983)" (*Action Inquiry* p215)

More recent theoretical support is provided by Mark Edwards's *Organisational Transformation for Sustainability* (2010).

Empirical support is relatively modest:

> "Two explicitly quantitative, empirical studies have now successfully quantified this developmental theory of organising in different ways. The first is [a] study of 10 organisations and their CEOs... (Rooke and Torbert 1998)... The second study (Leigh 2002) examined much larger companies from a much greater distance." (*Action Inquiry* p216)

Torbert's 2017 article for Integral Leadership Review, *The Pragmatic Impact on Leaders & Organizations Of Interventions Based in the Collaborative Developmental*

Action Inquiry Approach summarizes a lot of empirical research, including that of the current generation.

More recent empirical support on one aspect of the theory is provided by Laloux's *Reinventing Organisations*.

Support for the organisational action-logics by analogy comes from evidence for the existence of individual stages of development, and the patterns of behaviours of people at different stages:

> "The theoretical and empirical basis for discriminating among the personal action-logics... has a rich history. The individual action-logics... correspond closely to the developmental stages identified by developmental psychologists Skip Alexander (Alexander and Langer 1990), Bob Kegan (1982, 1994), Larry Kohlberg (1984), Jane Loevinger (Loevinger and Wessler 1970) and Ken Wilber (2000)." (See *Action Inquiry*, p210-215 for references to many empirical studies.)

The whole field is ripe for further research, for example on:

- Assessing an organisation's organisational action-logic. This paper is the first to propose a structured approach for this, but it is untested and there has been no research in this area.
- Different developmental lines of organisational action-logics, for example structure, management processes, information systems, conversations taking place, values and culture. Action Inquiry Fellow Jane Allen warns of trying to boil an organisation's action-logic down to a single measure. Reinventing Organisations is one of the few studies on any aspect of this.
- The relationship between individual, conversational and organisational action logics. The main study is Organisational Transformation as a Function of CEO's Developmental Stage (Rooke and Torbert 1998). Meaning Making and Management Effectiveness (Fisher, Merron and Torbert 1986) may also provide some pointers.

Developmental theory does make some testable predictions, as follows:

- Organisational redesigns may deliver short- and medium-term cost savings, or improvements in things like customer service, but significant, lasting performance improvements require development to a later action-logic.
- Organisations able to evolve to their next organisational action-logic – where they have introduced a new kind of conversation and succeeded in embedding it in their culture – will likely see significant, lasting improvement in effectiveness and performance.
- Success in implementing non-hierarchical, self-organising structure (one example is holocracy) requires the CEO to be at least at the

Redefining individual action-logic. (This condition is necessary but might not be sufficient.)

- Success in implementing teal practices requires the CEO to be at least at the Transforming individual action-logic.
- Success in implementing either holarchy or teal requires the introduction of new kinds of conversations. Imposing new processes and systems without introducing new kinds of conversations will fail to achieve the desired benefits of the processes and systems.
- Creating Peck's Community or Isaac's Dialogue needs the presence of someone at least at the Alchemical individual action-logic.

Comparison of terminologies

Different authors use different terminologies for developmental stages. Column 1 of Table 11.1 shows the organisational action-logic names used in *Action Inquiry* and this paper. Column 2 shows the corresponding individual action-logic names used in *Action Inquiry* and the *Harvard Business Review* article "Seven Transformations of Leadership". Column 3 shows the more recent names adopted by the Global Leadership Associates in their Global Leadership Profiles. This change responded to client feedback that the *Individualist* and *Strategist* names were misleading and unhelpful. Column 4 shows the names used by Joiner and Josephs in their book *Leadership Agility*. Columns 5 and 6 show the names used in Bob Kegan's work.

Columns 7 and 8 show the equivalent colours used in the Spiral Dynamics stage model, which applies to both individuals and groups. Column 7 shows the original colour names created by Beck and Cowan. Column 8 shows the revised colour scheme created by Wilber and used by Laloux. The pluses in the first and last row show this model has more than one stage here. Spiral Dynamics doesn't have a separate stage corresponding to *Expert* or *Experiments*. In Beck and Cowan's language, this would probably be blue-orange (i.e. early orange).

Further aspects

Table 11.1: comparison of terminologies

Org. A-L	Individual action-logics					Spiral Dynamics stages	
1. Action Inquiry	2. AI / HBR	3. GLA / GLP	4. J&J	5. Kegan early	6. Kegan later	7. B&C	8. W&L
Conception	Impulsive	Impulsive	Enthusiast+	First order consciousness	Impulsive mind	Purple+	Magenta+
Investments	Opportunist	Opportunist	Operator	Second order consciousness	Sovereign or Imperial mind	Red	Red
Incorporation	Diplomat	Diplomat	Conformer	Third order consciousness	Socialised mind	Blue	Amber
Experiments	Expert	Expert	Expert				
Systematic Productivity	Achiever	Achiever	Achiever	Fourth order consciousness	Self-authoring mind	Orange	Orange
Social Network	Individualist	Redefining	Catalyst			Green	Green
Collaborative Inquiry	Strategist	Transforming	Co-creator	Fifth order consciousness	Self-transform-ing mind	Yellow	Teal
Community of Inquiry	Alchemist	Alchemical	Synergist			Turquoise	Turquoise
Liberating Disciplines	Ironist	Ironic				Coral+	Indigo+

TWELVE

References and further reading

The first place to go is *Action Inquiry – The Secret of Timely and Transforming Leadership* by Bill Torbert and Associates (Berrett-Koehler, 2004). If you liked this work and want more information, *Action Inquiry* is a good starting point.

For people looking to jump from theory to practice at the later levels, to find in themselves the personal courage to fail that is needed at these later levels, recommended (after *Action Inquiry*) are:

- Torbert's *Creating a Community of Inquiry* (Wiley Interscience, 1976). This book gives a frank, first person account of vulnerability in action: it's hopes and doubts, joys and despairs, courage and flinching.
- *Focusing* by Eugene Gendlin (1978), which describes a technique for first-person action inquiry. This helps open up an awareness of the fourth territory of experience, an awareness that is required for transformation to *Alchemical* and *Level Eight*.

For insights into *Level Five (Systematic Productivity)*, see:

- *Jack – What I've Learned Leading a Great Company and Great People* by Jack Welch with John Byrne (Warner Books, 2001). GE under Jack Welch was perhaps an archetypal Systematic Productivity organisation and this autobiography is enjoyable, easy read.
- Any book on such subjects as Six-Sigma, Lean, ISO9001, quality management, balanced scorecards, Baldridge Performance Excellence, European Foundation for Quality Management, and so on.

For more information on *Level Six (Social Network)* and *Level Seven (Collaborative Inquiry)* see:

- *Reinventing Organizations: A Guide to Creating Organizations Inspired by the Next Stage in Human Consciousness* by Frederic Laloux (Nelson Parker, 2014).

For more information on *Level Eight (Foundational Community of Inquiry)* see:

- *The Different Drum* by M. Scott Peck (1987). A readable and accessible account (it has a quote by Carly Simon on the back) of the author's experiences of creating Communities.
- *Dialogue and the Art of Thinking Together* by William Isaacs (Doubleday, 1999). This is more structured, rigorous, and academic than *The Different Drum*, and consequently heavier going.
- Torbert's *Creating a of Community Inquiry* as described above.

For *Level Nine* (*Liberating Disciplines*) see Torbert's *The Power of Balance: Transforming Self, Society and Scientific Inquiry* (Sage, 1991) or, to a lesser extent, *Personal and Organisational Transformations* (Edgework Press, 1995).

The book also quotes some of Torbert's earlier work, including *Managing the Corporate Dream* (Dow Jones-Irwin, 1987). *Action Inquiry* largely supersedes this.

People interested in the academic, philosophical, psychological, and scientific bases of this model may wish to consult *Organisational Transformation for Sustainability – An Integral Metatheory* by Mark G. Edwards (Routlege, 2010). The book (based on Edwards's doctoral thesis) is for readers comfortable with the language of postgraduate academic writing. Torbert wrote the foreword, and he begins with:

"Once every generation or so, a field-defining scholarly statement appears. Mark Edwards's metatheory for organisational transformation is such a book for the field of organisational change and transformation. As demanding as it is of the reader (and it is no easy read), it ought to become a required touchstone for further theorising and research in organisational transformation. It is a comprehensive, appreciative, critical, creative revisioning of the field that helps all the members of that field locate themselves anew within it, helps them see the issues their own work has neglected, helps them reassess the scale of the field's challenges and helps them locate aspects of their field's literature that they may have heretofore altogether missed."

For more information on individual action-logics, see:
- Torbert's 2005 HBR article with David Rooke: *Seven Transformations of Leadership*. The article is a summary of *Action Inquiry*.
- Global Research Associates (www.gla.global) offers the Global Leadership Profile (GLP). The GLP is a diagnostic tool to identify which action-logics someone works from.
- The Centre for Creative Leadership (www.ccl.org) provides a range of tools, including Transformations™, a "flexible, user-friendly tool for self-understanding, coaching, leadership development, and culture development".

- Torbert's 2017 article for Integral Leadership Review, *The Pragmatic Impact on Leaders & Organizations Of Interventions Based in the Collaborative Developmental Action Inquiry Approach*
- *Leadership Agility* by Joiner and Josephs (Jossey-Bass, 2007) – a useful practical manual of what leadership means at the different action-logics, and a great companion to *Action Inquiry*.
- *In Over Our Heads – The Mental Demands of Modern Life* by Robert Kegan (Harvard University Press, 1994).

Printed in Great Britain
by Amazon